M000045119

JUMPSTART
your
CREATIVITY

JUMPSTART
your
CREATIVITY

—10 JOLTS—
TO GET CREATIVE
AND STAY CREATIVE

SHAWN DOYLE
AND
STEVEN ROWELL

© Copyright 2013–Shawn Doyle and Steven Rowell

All rights reserved. This book is protected by the copyright laws of the United States of America. This book may not be copied or reprinted for commercial gain or profit. The use of short quotations or occasional page copying for personal or group study is permitted and encouraged. Permission may be granted upon request.

Sound Wisdom
167 Walnut Bottom Road
Shippensburg, PA 17257
www.soundwisdom.com

This book and all other Sound Wisdom books are available at bookstores and distributors worldwide.

ISBN 13 TP: 978-1-937879-28-0

ISBN 13 Ebook: 978-1-937879-29-7

For Worldwide Distribution, Printed in the U.S.A.

1 2 3 4 5 6 7 8 9 10 /17 16 15 14 13

DEDICATIONS

FROM STEVEN TO:

Mom and Dad, thank you for loving me unconditionally and for all the sacrifices you made throughout the years to help me become the person I am today. Thank you for being such loving grandparents too. Ali and Farahnaz, thank you for your love and support. You inspire me to be a better person in so many ways. Dorothy, your spirit lives and fills the hearts of so many; may Kia bring you more great smiles, laughter, and never-ending joy!

My adventurous wife, Jamila, my anchor and my lighthouse, here's to living our dreams and to love, honor, cherish, adore, and edit! My son, you fill my heart and give me great joy and purpose in life every day. Head hug little mister! My big brother David, thank you for persevering and inspiring me to live a life of character.

My best friends Travis Mann and Mike Kennedy, thank you for listening all these years and still taking my phone calls. Adam Hommey, thank you for being you and never settling for less, ever. Glenn Gleason, I love you and miss you every day, R.I.P.

Finally, my mentors, teachers, and inspirations, Walter and Jayne Naff, Lambuth Tomlinson, Will Rogers, Dwight Sypolt, George Kalogridis, Leo Buscaglia, Sam Walton, Fred Smith, Joe Polish, Tom Antion, Andrew Ulichney, M.D., Greg Bogdanovich, Tom Peters, Tony Robbins, Michael Silver, M.D., Jack Canfield and Brendon Burchard, thank you for sharing your gifts, wisdom, and truth with me over the years.

FROM SHAWN TO:

Rachael, with all my love—I will always leave the light on for you!

CONTENTS

CHAPTER 1

IDEATION TECHNIQUES

*There is a fountain of youth: it is your
mind, your talents, the creativity you bring
to your life and the lives of people you love.
When you learn to tap this source, you will
truly have defeated age.*
—SOPHIA LOREN

WELCOME to *How to Skin a Badger!* (Oh sorry, that is the other book title we are working on.) Welcome to *Jumpstart Your Creativity!* Think of this book as a powerful generator with big jumper cables to give you ten jolts to fire up your creativity. I am Shawn Doyle and this is Steven Rowell, we are your creativity expert hosts.

In this day and age of information overload and cynicism with sound bites like "life would be great if...," "I'm just surviving," or "We used to, we used to...," *we* say there is great hope among us! Creativity abounds with fervor, zest, and zeal! All of the technology we take for granted today came from creative people who had the courage to pursue their dreams. The post-it note, the Segway, the iPhone, even the

100-miles-to-the-gallon hybrid car made by Philadelphia high school students were all made possible because of, yes—you're smart you guessed it—creativity.

Austrian daredevil Felix Baumgartner made the highest and fastest jump in history, leaping out of a helium balloon at an altitude of 128,100 feet, reaching a maximum speed of 833.9 miles per hour, or Mach 1.24, and safely landing on earth after a mile-long parachute ride. Future NASA astronauts will wear the identical suit that Baumgartner wore. This was made possible by the collaboration, expert science and math, and the creativity of more than 300 people including more than 70 engineers, scientists, and physicians who have been working for five years.

Most of us will never participate in such a creative, breakthrough, world-record-setting project (if you fall from a high distance, you really need to have a team of experts—don't try it at home). You may only have to be creative a few times each month—coming up with an alternate route during rush hour, new ways to get your kids to clean up their rooms, or creative financing to keep your lights on and a roof over your head, or a big project at work.

No matter how mundane or extraordinary our lives may seem to us, our ability to access greater creativity is one engine for innovation in our daily lives, hopefully to better our lives, our families, our communities, towns, countries, and some day the world (we are optimists)!

Creativity most often begins because of a grand idea or to overcome a problem, challenge, or obstacle. Peter Diamandis—founder of the X PRIZE Foundation, graduate of MIT and Harvard Medical School—and award-winning journalist Steven Kotler co-authored *Abundance*, which started with a big, hairy, audacious goal:

> Imagine a world of nine billion people with clean water, nutritious food, affordable housing, personalized education, top-tier medical care, and nonpolluting, ubiquitous energy. Building this better world is humanity's grandest challenge.

The hundreds of X PRIZE competitions completed to date have unleashed creativity, innovation, and sheer determination for problem solving in the most unlikely places and with the most unlikely of characters. We are inspired by Peter Diamandis, Steve Jobs, Walt Disney, Dr. Seuss, as well as average Joes and Sallys who embrace their creativity every day. We have written this book for every Joe, Sally, Tom, Enrique, Lakisha, Yu, Rufus, and Caius who know deep in their heart of hearts they have creativity inside of them, can remember it from their childhood, and yearn to let it out once again.

Imagine a book on creativity that has no fluff, never wastes your time, is fun to read and gives you exact steps to generate better ideas, evaluate these ideas, and get better results! We embrace this big idea and hope that you benefit from our gift to you. We know that 91 percent of all people who buy a book never read more than the first chapter, so we have packed this first chapter with immediate actionable strategies on how to come up with new ideas using brainstorming that works. It's called *ideation*, and we'll show you how to use it right now.

WHO WE ARE

First, to get a little business out of the way so you understand who is talking to you in this book and why we are qualified to teach you about creativity, we offer you our quick bios. *Shawn* (he is waving on the right but you can't see him as he is outside the margin) has been a trainer, book author, consultant, and cartoonist for more than two decades (more than he likes to admit...shhh, he's 54). He has written fourteen books at the time of this writing, and is writing three more as you read these words. Shawn has resilience and discipline seldom seen and a generous spirit that inspires every audience. He is truly motivated by helping others improve their lives. *Steven* (he is waving on the left) has been a trainer, speaker, consultant, and book author for many years as well. He used to work for The Walt Disney World Co., (talk about creative!) and is known in many circles as the "Idea Doctor," a name given to him by his clients that has stuck with him. He's a serial entrepreneur, classic ADD/ADHD, bright-shiny-object idea machine with a huge heart for helping others.

Many people tell us individually that we are "the most creative people they know." Since we are both creative maniacs and we teach creativity in corporate and nonprofit classrooms across the United States, we feel somewhat qualified to help you jumpstart your creativity. So let's move beyond the resume propaganda and into what you really care about—learning how to be more creative. (Note: our publisher's legal department objected to the term "propaganda" and asked us to take it out, but we thought it was really cool; so being the creative rebels that we are, we stuck it back into the final manuscript and hope they don't notice.)

This book does *not* have the proverbial required introductory chapter that tells you what we are going to tell you. We figured we would show you some respect and just go ahead and cut right to the chase.

"THIS IS YOUR BRAIN."

Okay, just in case you were thinking literally, the line above is not actually your brain—it is the title of this section. After traveling around the country teaching people how to be more creative, we realized most people approach creativity different from the way your brain really works. For example: I mention the word frog, you think: *Green, which reminds you of the grass on a golf course, speaking of golf, boy last week George really got plastered on the 16th hole, speaking of plaster I probably need to repair that hole in the wall that is there because I took that big mirror down and I need to remember to stop at the hardware store to buy some plaster; you know when I think of plaster it makes me think of the old days when people would put plaster on somebody's skin to remove disease—some people call that "plaster."*

No, this is not the ramblings of an insane person, this is how most people really think. Most of us do not think in a linear way: 1,2,3,4,5,6,7,8,9. We think more in terms of connections and associations as in that run-on sentence about the frog. In fact you could connect them in the following ways: golf-George-plastered-repair-old days. That is how our brain really works, a loose series of connected associations that are all somehow related to one another.

Think of it as a spider web, a fishing net, a pinball machine, or Lady Gaga's "meat dress" (okay maybe the last one was not a good example—sorry for being a little too creative), but if you think of a web or a net, each string or strand goes from point to point. Are you with us so far? The point is, most people conduct brainstorming or ideation in a way that is not linked to how the brain actually works. The processes of brainstorming are often way too linear and that's why too often they don't work at all!

We pile people into a conference room, pull out a marker and a flip-chart and say, "Okay people, let's generate some ideas!" Most people we talk to detest brainstorming. Why do they detest brainstorming? We hear many reasons. Most of them are say, "It is highly ineffective and awkward," or in the majority of cases, "The person facilitating the brainstorming does not do a good job." Another common complaint is that people too often make comments or judgments aloud in response to others' contributions during the brainstorming and this shuts some participants down, keeping them from contributing any more to the discussion.

Our goal in this book is to help you understand tools, tips, techniques, and approaches you can apply today to help you generate better ideas, evaluate them and get better results.

WHY ARE YOU READING THIS BOOK?

Why are you interested in jumpstarting your creativity? Why are your jumper cables out to begin with? Why do you need a jolt to get you going in terms of creativity? Why do we ask why? Because we know that you will get a lot more out of the book if you have identified the reason you want to learn about creativity in the first place. Your reasons may include:

- I am not creative, but I want to learn to be more creative.

- I'm already creative and would like to be more creative.

- I haven't studied very much about creativity and would like to understand more.

- I need to be more creative at work and this will help me generate better results.

- I have to get more creative with my dates or I may never get married.

- I need to be more creative with my children and help them stay creative.

- My life isn't working right now, and I'm finally ready to fix it.

- My wife said I need to read it.

- My dog said I need to read it.

- My cat downloaded the book on my e-reader so I figured I might as well read it.

So what is your goal? Some of the goals you have may be in this list, and some may not.

Write the reasons you are reading this book and why you want to jumpstart your creativity. If you are reading this on an e-reader of any kind, please do not write on the screen with a marker. Please write your reasons on a piece of paper with a pen, marker, or pencil.

Now circle your "Top 2 or 3" that are the most important and urgent. Circle the ones that have the greatest potential to make a difference in your work or your life.

Now that we have determined your "why" for creativity and you know what you want to work on, the rest of this chapter is designed to give you tools, tips, and approaches for generating new and unique ideas.

---

cre·a·tiv·i·ty [kree-ey-tiv-i-tee, kree-uh-]

noun

1. the ability to transcend traditional ideas, rules, patterns, relationships, or the like, and to create meaningful new ideas, forms, methods, interpretations, etc.; originality, progressiveness, or imagination: the need for creativity in modern industry; creativity in the performing arts.

2. the process by which one utilizes creative ability.

Before we go further, one quick word of caution: the process of ideating is extremely messy and imprecise—it is a mix of science and art. Ideating is a big hot mess, and you often end up with a massive collection of ideas. When you review these ideas you will find there are some horrible ideas, some not-so-horrible ideas, some really stupid ideas, some good ideas, and a few brilliant ideas. Keep in mind that during the ideation phase you are not making judgments about the quality of the ideas—your goal should be to develop as many ideas as possible. It's about quantity not quality at this stage. Having lots of ideas helps generate more ideas. It's a catalytic process. When Steven and I brainstorm a book, project, program, or a product, we come up with a multiplicity of ideas, probably too many. We both realize the more ideas we come up with, the more these ideas multiply, and we come up with other ideas.

IDEATION MATERIALS

Many people often ask us this question, "Where do you come up with all of these ideas?" Our answer is usually something like, "They just come to us." When people who aren't creative or who want to be more creative hear us say that an "idea just comes to us," they are often mystified and sometimes frustrated wishing they could say the same thing. It often sounds to people as though the ideas fell out of the sky and into our laps. So we do not say, "The ideas just come to us." What we do say is, "Both of us, over our entire careers as both employees of corporate America and as serial entrepreneurs, have developed a set of tools and approaches that help us develop ideas and concepts quickly." So how can you find ideas and information?

First, we want to encourage you to be aware of information and stimulation and ideas that are continually circulating around you. Often the information circulating around you at work and at home can be a source of inspiration. If you pay attention and are observant, you will see, touch, smell, and hear information that can be a stimulus for an idea. Shawn once received a catalog for Restoration Hardware. He was so inspired by this catalog that he wrote an article about it. Below is a short excerpt from that article:

> I went out to the mailbox to get my mail this afternoon. I sat down for a light lunch and was sorting the mail, not knowing that I would come across something that was absolutely amazing. I reached into the stack and pulled out the latest Restoration Hardware catalog. I opened the front cover and was immediately pulled in to a new world. Inside the cover was an impassioned message from the CEO with an amazing picture of him wearing a leather jacket. As I turned the pages I realized that I was not looking at the catalog but I was looking at a work of art, and I was amazed at the quality of the photos, the layout and the extraordinary way all of the products were arranged in each picture. It reminded me of a brochure from a world-class art museum. As I sat slack-jawed looking through the glossy pages I started thinking. Has a catalog ever amazed me before? No. Have I ever been fascinated by a catalog before? No. Have I ever considered a catalog a work of art before? No. What is it that made that catalog so amazing? As I contemplated this over my lunch I realized what it was—it was extraordinary.

Often there are things that you come across or are exposed to that can have an impact on you creatively, but you have to be alert enough to notice it.

So here are a few tips from the creative team to help you be a better observer and creator:

Open your eyes.

Wherever you are, make sure to look at what's going on around you. We often have the experience of saying to someone when walking in a city, "Hey did you notice that clown back there doing a handstand on the unicycle juggling oranges?" The typical response is, "Where did you see that?" Come on, open your eyes people! We know the typical routine is to walk with your eyes looking down, make no connection with other people, and listen to the music playing on your iPod. With this routine, you are missing out on stimulus that may help generate your next best idea. But don't beat yourself up for this. An interesting 1999 Harvard University study, "Gorillas in our Midst" by Daniel Simons and Christopher Chabris coined the terms "inattentional blindness" and "change blindness." The idea is that people often miss seeing large changes in their visual field, even if these changes are significant enough to be easily noticed if one is expecting them. Filling out forms at the doctor's office without reading them, realizing "everybody has a car just like mine" the day after you purchase your new car (these cars were always around you, you just didn't realize it), and missing a clown in the road when you are staring down the street are all examples of how easy it is for us to miss these things with our eyes.

Read.

Oh well, thank you, you guys are geniuses—I should read? Wow, that's a new one. But we have a very specific suggestion about reading. If you want to become more creative and more innovative and better at generating ideas, don't just read fiction like most people. Read biographies about creative people. Read biographies about inventors and artists. Read about architects, jugglers, circus performers, sideshows, explorers, astronauts, movie directors. We're not saying that fiction can't stimulate your creativity, but nonfiction work is often laced throughout with new ideas, approaches, and inspiration. So we recommend a mix of fiction and nonfiction books about creative people, creative ideas, creative lives, and, of course, how to be more creative. If you read a book about the building of the Eiffel Tower, you can't help but be stimulated with the amazing creativity and innovation that was involved in building the tower (at least if you're paying attention that is).

Change up.

If you normally read magazines about engineering or project management, you have our sympathies (okay that was a joke), but if you normally read magazines about your industry, go to the newsstand or download to your e-reader magazines that you normally don't read. Getting outside of your normal reading and viewing habits can certainly stimulate your creativity.

Watch new.

The popularity of the new sources for video viewing has been a boon to people who are creative. Why is that? Well, often both of us spot documentaries on Netflix or on Amazon that we would've never known about in the past nor would they have been available. With a quick click, you can download any number of documentaries, television shows, or movies that you never had access to before. These can be tremendously stimulating to your creativity. The same approach can work by looking for videos online on sites such as You-Tube in order to stimulate your creativity.

Don't dismiss.

Too many times when we see something that is viewed as creative or as a little bit different we have a tendency to dismiss it. Think about popular acts that are currently playing across the country at the writing of this book. The Blue Man group has many shows in several cities that are all highly successful. Cirque du Soleil has dozens of shows playing around the world, almost all of them highly successful. However, we are both completely convinced that in the early days of The Blue Man Group, people probably thought they were wacky and that they would never be successful. The same is true for Cirque du Soleil. How do you possibly explain either one of them to someone who has never seen them—it is difficult at best. A circus with no animals? Three blue men? But yet both of these shows are so creative and so amazing that they have been very successful. Even if something is not successful, it still is a good idea for you to pay attention to it because it might give you new and different ideas that you can apply to your own life or work.

Keep a morgue.

We know that you're shocked by this suggestion as you certainly are not a medical examiner or a funeral director!

So what the heck is a morgue? Back in the old days, professional cartoonists used to keep what they called a "morgue." What is a morgue for a cartoonist? It was simply pictures that they had cut out of magazines and newspapers and filed them for future reference. So if a cartoonist was drawing a frog for example, he or she would simply look in their F files for pictures of frogs. Why does a cartoonist need a picture of a frog? Well it's very simple, it is easier to draw a frog when looking at a picture of a real one (this was before the Internet). Consequently, a cartoonist would have thousands of pictures of anything you can imagine that would be required to draw in a cartoon. It could be a picture of a crab or a camel or a Cadillac. The pictures were important reference points to draw cartoons that looked like what they were trying to depict.

So what would be your version of a morgue? It could be a notebook or a file that you physically drop images into or an electronic collection that you can access when needed. The idea is to collect images, articles, fabric, whatever materials stimulate your creativity. We think of this as "idea harvesting." The harvest goes into your morgue. You could tear pages out of a catalog, put in a note from a legal pad, drop in a greeting card that someone gave you, or a napkin from the restaurant you went to while on a business trip. You define what "they" are—if they inspire you or stimulate your creativity, they go into your morgue. We are sure by now you've probably figured out the way that a morgue is used; when in the process of creativity, you pull out your physical or electronic morgue file and look it over. Hopefully something there will stimulate a creative idea.

DISPLAYED THINKING

Before we cover the ideation techniques, there's one other key component that we need to review with you. This is known as *displayed thinking*. Anytime you are in the midst of a creative activity for generating ideas or creative solutions, you need to make sure to write those on a whiteboard or flip chart (or the wall) so that everyone can see the answers. How does displayed thinking help in the creative process? Well simply put, it allows each person in the group to see the ideas as they are recorded, and that helps them know what has been said and they can also feed off the ideas that are being displayed. If those ideas were written on a small legal pad where only a few people could see them, it does not work nearly as well. So don't make the fatal mistake of not writing the ideas in a place where everybody in the group working on the ideas can see them. Display the thinking on a white board or flip chart.

IDEATION TECHNIQUES

There are several different ideation techniques you can use to generate ideas. What we are asking you *not* to do is brainstorm. We believe that the era of effective brainstorming is over because we say so (just kidding); in all seriousness, we think that brainstorming has lost its effectiveness because it has been overdone and poorly done. Most people, when invited to a brainstorming session, are not exactly thrilled. When there are so many other great techniques out there aside from brainstorming, why use the one that's the senior citizen falling apart and on life support?

One cautionary point regarding ideation with groups is the importance of avoiding "group think." Group think can surface when groups are brainstorming or discussing issues. Group think occurs in several ways such as the group depending too heavily on consensus-based group decisions to the point that individual creativity and contribution is minimized or missed altogether, letting individual biases or viewpoints, especially from high-influence group members, keep others from sharing their ideas or causing them to unfortunately modify their statements to be accepted by the group even though their authentic statement might be in contrast to the discussion.

IDEATION TIPS

- Smaller groups working together is better than trying to ideate with a large group of participants—6 to 8 is ideal, 9 to 12 is tough, 13 and more a hot mess.

- To avoid group think, instead of relying solely on open discussion and sharing ideas aloud by group members, you may want to have each person write down their thoughts on a piece of paper and turn them in—the facilitator may or may not post all of the responses at that time, it depends on the goal of that session.

- Make sure you have "the right people" in the room. We mean make sure you have all areas represented, all levels of the organization contributing, or all of the subject matter experts who should be involved—ideation in a vacuum results in less-than-best results.

At the end of this chapter you will see our recommended "Rules for Ideation." Now let's dig into thirteen of our more than fifty ways to come up with new ideas through ideation.

Ideation Technique Number 1: Reverse Brainstorming

Reverse Brainstorming is exactly the same as regular brainstorming except there is a unique twist. Remember we asked you not to brainstorm the old way. Let's say we work for the Billings Bowling Ball company. We get together with our team to brainstorm a way to increase sales and revenue. So the objective as stated is to "increase sales and revenue." Instead of brainstorming the old way, we're going to use Reverse Brainstorming; instead of talking about how to increase sales and revenue, we will brainstorm a list of the opposite or the reverse, which is "how *not* to increase sales and revenue." This focus frees up everyone to be highly creative to figure out how *not* to meet the objective. We have conducted this exercise with hundreds of groups and they always have a lot of fun figuring out ways to mess up everything. Once several flip chart pages of ideas have been written down, then of course we look at all of the ways not to increase sales and revenue and ask ourselves what the opposite of those would be. This is a highly effective technique for generating a ton of ideas. We have another name for Reverse Brainstorming—"What is the dumbest thing you could do?" When we remove the restraint of what can be done it tends to encourage people's creativity.

Ideation Technique Number 2: Random Stimulation

Have you ever been riding a bicycle, working out, or even taking a shower and you came up with a great idea that seemed like it was out of the blue? Sure, all of us have. We, however, do not believe the idea was "out of the blue"—it was stimulated by something. It may have been the image on the shampoo bottle, a graphic on the gym wall, or seeing what you saw when riding your bicycle around the marina. It was that spider web/fish net of a brain of yours firing off connections and ideas.

Unconsciously you saw, touched, heard, or felt something that stimulated that idea. This is the phenomenon known as Random Stimulation. Some outside external stimulus or stimuli randomly triggered your brain to generate an idea. Using this as an ideation technique, we can use one of several approaches to get our brain to randomly generate ideas and then also do this in a meeting room.

Approach 1

Simply go to Google and click on the Google image tab. Once there, choose various words at random. We might put in "squid" and then look at all the pictures the word squid generates. Print out one or two images generated by the word squid. Then pick another word at random such as "architect." Pick two images under the architect category and print them

18

out as well. After you go through a series of ten random words and have printed pictures, these are used as a Random Stimulation exercise.

Here's how it would work in a group setting. We would say to the group, "We are currently trying to figure out a way of increasing sales and revenue" (from the bowling ball company example). Now we ask the group to set that problem aside and look at a stack of random images. When looking at the images the group members are only to say what those images remind them of, as a facilitator writes down the phrases and words they mention.

After a large list of words have been generated from the random photos, you ask the group if any of the words on the list remind them of a solution to the problem. You would be amazed how many times we hear people say, "Oh that reminds me of something! What if we did this?" The biggest challenge of the Random Stimulation approach is getting people to believe a tool that seems completely arbitrary, random, and somewhat abstract is useful in generating ideas. We have seen this approach work many times. Have we ever seen this approach not work? Of course, but the main reason it doesn't work, in most cases, is the fact that the group does not believe the approach will work, so they do not open themselves up to the possibilities because they had shut down before they even started.

Approach 2

This technique is exactly the same as mentioned in Approach 1, the only difference is the source material for the ideas. In this approach each person brings one or two random magazines or catalogs to the meeting. A person selects a catalog, closes his or her eyes, flips through pages, then points to one of the pages. The facilitator asks what is under the finger, either a word or a picture. The facilitator writes the word or the picture on the flip chart and then follows the same process as outlined in Approach 1. The key to this approach is making sure there are a variety of magazines from which to choose.

Random Stimulation is an effective technique. It has been rumored that this technique has been used effectively in Hollywood and New York in both film and television production for years. For example, a creative team could sit around and combine different words in order to come up with an idea for a show that was new or different. Someone could say "playboy and lifeguards," and of course that would be the television show "Baywatch." According to sources that's exactly how the show was pitched to the network—"playboy lifeguards." You could combine two words such as millionaire and hillbillies and come up, of course, with the "Beverly Hillbillies." You could combine the ventriloquist and automobile and come up with the TV show "Knight Rider" (we refuse at this point to comment on the mentality of American television), so you get the idea.

Ideation Technique Number 3: The Rules

Often we find organizations have rules in place that have been in place for a long time. These rules served their purposes well during the time they were enacted, but may have outgrown their usefulness and may be holding the organization

New Perspectives Tips:

- Read trade journals from different industries from your own.

- Try new things—visit other companies, watch different documentaries, interview people in other industries.

- Ask yourself, *Beyond my industry, who else has dealt with similar problems and challenges—how did they address them?*

- Find and talk to people who think differently—military/civilian, engineer/artist, construction worker/dancer, athlete/librarian.

back. So the idea behind this technique is to write a list of all of the rules an organization has (they could be about marketing, sales, design, etc.). And then figure out if those rules were to change, how would it change the ideas. For example, we just recently read an article about Applewood Farms, an organic meat producer that has grown successfully over the past twenty-five years. One of the defining moments of the CEO's history is when he realized that the company did not have to be in the meat production business. They re-worked one of their own rules that said they didn't have to have a manufacturing facility—they could contract out that part of the process. That was a defining moment for the company. Think of some of the rules that have dominated industries over the past several decades:

- Radio as local (nope)

- Movies are watched at a movie theater (hello Netflix)

- Books are a physical product (guess again)

- You have to go to college to go to college (wrong)

- Businesses must have a brick and mortar presence (laughable)

- Music has a physical form such as a CD (can you say download)

- Data is stored on your computer (hello cloud)

- Pizza is cooked in an oven (hi microwave)

- To find someone to date, you have to go to a club or a church (can you say e-Harmony)

- You play games on a game system (ha!)

- Yogurt is in a cup (wrong again—GoGurt is in a tube)

Business opportunities are based on rules and assumptions. But if you can make a list of all of your rules and assumptions and then figure out if they are still relevant and have never been questioned, then you may have the basis for the next great idea—or several of them.

Ideation Technique Number 4: Blank Slate

The idea behind the Blank Slate technique is to remove all restrictions, limitations, and budgets from the ideation process. Come up with an objective, and then say to the group, "If we were starting today from scratch and had no limitations on structure, finances, or logistics, in other words if we were starting from a blank piece of paper, how would we handle this problem, challenge, or situation?" When there are no limits, people tend to become a lot more creative and innovative. Once the list is built, then have the group go back and look over the solutions to see if any of them would actually work.

Ideation Technique Number 5: The Consulting Team

Using this technique, have the group create a list of various celebrities. The celebrities need to be from all areas including sports, entertainment, literature, and art. Also make sure that they picked both current and celebrities from the past including those from history. Once the list is developed, pick a dozen names from the list, which are a mix of both current and past celebrities. Then pose the problem and ask, "How would this situation be handled by..."

- Donald Trump

- Lady Gaga

- Muhammad Ali

- Bette Midler

- Napoleon

- Louis Armstrong

- Gustave Eiffel

- Renoir

- Thomas Edison

- Madam Curie

- Hillary Clinton

- Ronald Reagan

- Big Bird

- Donald Duck

- Plato

The group has a lot of fun coming up with how each celebrity would handle the problem, opportunity, or challenge. The best way to conduct the exercise is to have the team members consider each celebrity one at a time and talk about how that person would handle it. Often groups laugh and snicker during this exercise, which seems to border on being ridiculous. After the list has all been written out as to how each celebrity would handle those situations or problems, the group then reviews to see if some of them would make any sense. This can be a very effective tool for getting out of your own way and thinking about a problem or situation from very different viewpoints.

Ideation Technique Number 6: What if this was?

The idea behind this exercise is to talk about how a problem, opportunity, or challenge would be handled if it was treated as being something else entirely. How does this exercise work? We simply make a list in advance (feel free to use our list below) and then ask the group how they would handle it if it were as described. For example, let's say we are trying to gain market share from a competitor. If we asked the group, "How would you treat this if it was a war?" The answers are much different from asking, "How would you handle this if it was a social movement?" It always amazes us how the answers change dramatically when people look at the problem in a completely different and unique way. Here is a suggested list of some of the what-ifs:

- What if it was a war?

- What if it was a movement?

- What if there was an exclusive club?

- What if it was a rare collectible?

- What if it was a party?

- What if it was a dance rave?

- What if it was a celebration?

- What if there was a charitable cause?

- What if it was a patriotic event?

- What if it was an unveiling?

- What if there was a space rocket launch?

- What if it was a visit by state dignitaries?

- What if it was a pep rally?

- What if it was a car show?

- What if it was a football game?

- What if it was a chess match?

Obviously the solutions and ideas from each of these would be remarkable and different. That is the idea and the power of this technique.

Ideation Technique Number 7: Word Chain

This technique is an idea using words as a way of generating ideas through the technique of word association. Simply put, one person in the group starts with a word and says that word out loud. The next person in the group then has to say a word that reminds him or her of that word. Each word that has spoken out loud needs to be written on a flip chart by the facilitator. So for example, someone says "frog," another person says "hop," another person says "beer," and then we end up with a word chain consisting of: frog, hop, beer, golden, retriever, collector, taxes, Rome, gladiator, fight, gloves, winter, snow, ice, cream, cone, pine tree, floor cleaner, wood, mop, the Beatles, England, the queen, rock band.

Obviously once that entire list has been written on the chart, the group then reviews the list of words to see if there is something on that list that could be possibly aligned with or would help solve the problem, opportunity, or the challenge.

Ideation Technique Number 8: Crunchy Cheese Curls

Buy a large bag of crunchy cheese curls and bring it with you to meet with the group. Break the group into smaller groups and pour a bowl of crunchy cheese curls for each group. Identify the objective that you are working on. Have members of each group pull out a cheese curl one at a time and write down what the particular shape of that cheese curl reminds them of. It is very important that you purchase crunchy cheese curls and not just the soft kind. The soft kind all have the same shape, the crunchy kind have many unique shapes. It's kind of like looking at the shapes of clouds and imagining what they are. An additional benefit of this exercise is that you now have snacks as well as a way to stimulate your creativity!

Ideation Technique Number 9: Dead Silence

Purchase a bunch of colorful, small sticky pads and put them on the table. State the objective of the ideation and then ask each person to be completely and totally silent for a period of seven minutes; during that time each person is to individually write down potential solutions on their 3 x 5 sticky note. After the seven-minute period of absolute silence, ask each person to post their sticky note on the wall, and then review each one—one at a time in random order. Generally we find this exercise to be incredibly helpful as it is very rare when people are completely and totally silent. There is often a lot going on when people are trying to ideate. We have both found that we tend to generate great ideas when flying on planes. Our theory is that the reason why planes are so effective is that they are often quiet, and we are isolated from interruptions and noises. So we have purchased a plane just for the purposes of ideation. (Just kidding.)

Did You Know?

Post-It Notes® were discovered as a result of a mistake? Actually it was a failed invention that created Post-It Notes. Spencer Silver, a researcher at 3M, was working on a new heavy duty adhesive, but the substance he created was weaker than any adhesive they had at the time. Years later, in 1980, Arthur Frey, a 3M engineer, needed a solution for keeping his choir hymnal bookmarks to stick on the pages, and they worked well. So an executive assistant passed samples around the 3M office to other assistants and they began to use them on folders, reports, and contracts. When the 3M product development team presented the idea to the executive team, executives realized they had been using them for months and loved them. The idea was approved and are now available in 27 sizes, 57 colors, and 20 fragrances, resulting in $1 billion of sales for 3M alone. There are 19 other companies now making copy-cat notepads with their combined sales exceeding $1 billion.

Ideation Technique Number 10: Wacky Hero

Using this technique we get a little crazy and add some humor to the equation by asking a group to have the problem, situation, or challenge solved by a fictitious hero. Once we state the objective, we give the group a list of fictitious heroes and ask them how these heroes would solve the problem. The funny part is that people are puzzled and fascinated by the names of the heroes, and they have to not only figure out what the hero does (what their super powers are), but how this hero would theoretically solve the problem. Here is a list of our fictitious heroes—but hey, this is a book on creativity so feel free to make up your own list if you like. After people have reviewed each super hero and come up with a list of potential solutions, get back together as a group and discuss.

- Butterman
- Green Beany Man
- Blobbo
- Blue Hopper
- Mush Man
- Oil Girl
- Fox Flipper
- Silver Sue
- Waddle Woman
- Trendy Man
- Cloud Rider
- Super Squid
- Underboy
- Mighty Dust Mite
- Wonder Blunder
- Stinger Clown

Ideation Technique Number 11: Need(s) Not Being Met

Dr. Phil McGraw, the "Dr. Phil" on television and Oprah's former co-host, is now famous for the question, "How's that workin' for ya?" And most of the time people respond to his question, at least on his TV show, with, "Well, it's not workin' for me."

This ideation technique is great when working to come up with new solutions or enhancements for an existing product, service, or system. Let's take a look at the shower stall and shower head in your bathroom (hypothetically). When thinking of your current shower stall and shower head in your bathroom at home, what needs are not being met right now?

For example, you might say:

- Not safe—water gets too hot too quickly—it's dangerous and scalds me

- Not enough shower heads (comes up again in a moment)

- Not staying dry when I turn it on—shower head rotates toward the door and I get splashed with ice cold water when I first turn it on (it used to never do this)

- Not easy to clean

- Not enough shelf space

- No place to hang my loofa sponge

- Drain is way too slow

- Water spills out onto carpet way too easily

- Not enough overhead lighting for nighttime

- Not enough space—can't be in there with my spouse, too tight to wash my dog

- Not relaxing—no music, no seat, no massage jets, only one shower head (this triggers the thought, "Not comfortable")

One great opportunity from this exercise is shown in the final example, "Not relaxing." By identifying the need that is not being met currently, such as relaxing, you realize there are a host of issues related to this one issue, such as no music, no seat, not enough jets or shower heads; and it prompts you to think about the lack of comfort as well.

Research has shown that for most of us, it is easier and faster to look at something critically and identify what is wrong or missing, rather than find the good or what is right about something.

Once you have come up with your list of the "Needs Not Being Met" by this product, service, system, or situation, you can then start to look at 1) which of these needs are my most urgent and important to address; 2) which need(s) must be met and soon; and finally 3) what do I/we have to stop doing, start doing, or continue doing to get my needs met.

Ideation Technique Number 12: Pillars

Another ideation technique is designed to prompt your creativity by taking you through a series of pillars. The first five pillars were popularized by Jim Collins' life work on what makes companies great, found in his groundbreaking books, *Built to Last* and *Good to Great*. The rest of these pillars have been identified by our audiences over the past several years. Some pillars won't help your situation, so simply skip them.

The pillars are: Service; Quality; Cost; Growth; People; Efficiency; Productivity; Safety.

One example for this ideation technique is a team who is working through all of the issues related to whether or not we purchase new uniforms for our employees. Notice this ideation technique especially helps in the decision-making process. The ideation facilitator will write these words in two columns on a flip chart or dry erase board, and all participants will have a blank piece of paper in front of them. The participants will write each pillar down and then list their ideation issues underneath that pillar.

The facilitator will remind everyone of the specifics of the topic "new uniforms" and then read aloud the first pillar.

For example, after the papers are collected at the end, you might find the following results:

Quality:

- Buy uniforms that will last.

- Don't buy cheap uniforms.

- I hope we get uniforms that last more than three months.

- Get better uniforms, our current ones wear out in the armpits too fast.

- I'd rather have the company buy me three sets of high quality uniforms rather than five sets of cheaply made, low-cost uniforms.

- If the company would buy better quality uniforms I'm fine with them giving me three sets and then I buy any more sets myself.

- Please don't put the patches with our names on the shirts, it looks tacky and makes us look less professional.

- I sure hope we do a fashion show and bring in five or six options, letting folks vote for the one they think is the best quality and best fit for the work they do.

- We better test wash the uniforms we are considering because a few years ago the shirts lost their color fast and we looked horrible for a whole year.

- Let's buy uniforms that are machine washable but have that "wrinkle free" technology in them so our folks' uniforms look clean and pressed every day.

After the ideation process, then the team can go through a consensus exercise to determine the most important factors and decision-making criteria.

THE RULES

Yes we know it's funny to talk about rules in a book about creativity. But there are a few rules that are absolutely essential in making sure the ideation process is successful. Whenever you are working with a group generating ideas and solutions, make sure to state the rules upfront before you start. Designate someone in the group as Rule Enforcer to make sure the rules are enforced.

Rule 1. Have fun. We have learned from working with many of our clients that the more fun the client is having the more creative they can be and the more ideas flow.

Rule 2. No judgment. When people are generating ideas, the ideas may be good, bad, or brilliant. But the worst thing that can happen during the ideation phase is for someone to start judging the ideas as they are being developed. This will immediately destroy all of the creativity in the room.

Rule 3. No negativity. When people make negative comments and say negative things like, "That won't work," then they are going to kill the creative environment. Do not allow this to happen under any circumstances (okay, we know that was a little negative, but it was necessary).

Rule 4. Do not evaluate while you create. The creativity process and evaluation process should be separated with time and distance. Don't evaluate while you are trying to create. That should be a separate, distinct process that happens later.

Rule 5. Have an open mind. Too often it is the close-minded people of the world who refuse to be creative and they ruin creative endeavors. Encourage your people to have open minds and to consider all of the possibilities available to them. That is one of the benchmarks of creativity.

So now we have given you twelve different techniques for coming up with ideas. Would you like more? The good news is we have more than fifty different ways for generating ideas—you can access these by simply going to www.creativitylaunchpad.com.

EMBRACE ACCIDENTS FOR SUCCESS

The following inventions or discoveries came randomly or by way of accidents:

- Corn Flakes
- Microwave Ovens
- Silly Putty
- Play-Doh
- Mauve Dye
- Sweet 'n Low

- Potato Chips

- Fireworks

- Plastic

- Warfarin (Coumadine)

- Rogaine

- NutraSweet

- Penicillin

- Teflon

- Viagra

- Smart Dust

- Slinky

- Pacemaker

- Scotchgard

- LSD

- Inkjet Printers

- X-rays

- Goodyear

- Vulcanized Rubber

When you make room for accidents and random discoveries, you free up everyone to engage in greater creativity that leads to far superior innovation and much better results.

The following is a brief list of sources that continue to inspire both of us each and every month. As a disclaimer, please note that we are not being paid or compensated to endorse or to promote any of these products, goods, or services. These are examples that you might want to check out that may inspire you.

Magazines

- *Fast Company* often features amazing articles about people who were thinking very creatively.

- *Inc.* often features some crazy entrepreneur who is approaching a business in an entirely a new way.

- *Wired:* you would think this is a magazine about computers and technology, and in one sense you are right, but in another sense you would be wrong. It's about how technology is applied creatively to the world at large.

- *Psychology Today* has lots of ideas about the mind.

- *Vogue:* want to see the best pictures in fashion? Talk about creativity!

- *Entrepreneur* has lots of cool ideas about what business people are doing and thinking.

- *Success* is full of ideas that come from all over the place within inspiring collections of success stories.

Websites

- www.ted.com—Site of conferences with "ideas worth spreading."

- www.Google.com/images—Go to Google and click on the tab for Google images; put in a word like cotton candy and watch a universe of images open up to stimulate your imagination.

- www.huffingtonpost.com—Look at the art or culture section to see cutting-edge things that are occurring in the world of the visual arts or in the world of culture.

- www.thedailybeast.com—Daily Beast is a wild mix of story and other stuff.

- www.restorationhardware.com—Restoration hardware; trust us, it's amazing.

- www.artspan.com—Artists...lots of artists.

- www.michaelgraves.com—Home of architect and designer Michael Graves.

- www.youtube.com—In case you have lived in a cave somewhere, YouTube is packed with videos—search "inattentional blindness," "change blindness."

- www.thefuntheory.com—Can you change behavior easier if it is fun?

- www.etsy.com—Marketplace for crafters to sell their arts.

- www.kickstarter.com—Innovations, start-up, and causes looking for crowd funding.

For more magazines, websites, and creative resources, go to www.creativitylaunchpad/jumpstart.

So this brings us to the end of Chapter 1, our friend. In the next chapter we will talk about why there is a crisis in creativity. At the end of each chapter you will find a "Workit" page. This section is designed to help you stop and think about what you just read. It will help you determine your strengths and the areas where you need improvement. It also allows you to take notes and to create action plans to build each area of creativity.

WORK IT

Which ideation technique are you most likely going to use first and why?

_____

_____

_____

_____

_____

_____

What are some of the issues you could work on right away—at work, at home, or within yourself—that would benefit greatly from ideation?

_____

_____

_____

_____

_____

_____

When are you going to schedule your first ideation experience and who needs to be invited?

_____

_____

_____

_____

_____

_____

What are the benefits or the value of making and taking the time to follow through on an ideation experience? How will your work life or personal life be better for it? (What will inspire you to take action right now?)

_____

_____

_____

_____

_____

_____

_____

CREATIVITY CRISIS

The thing is to become a master and in your
old age to acquire the courage to do what
children did when they knew nothing.
—Ernest Hemingway

WAKE up! We are in a crisis mode for creativity in our nation. Sadly due to our current education system still being so focused on functional literacy since the industrial revolution, the creativity with which we are born is basically trained out of us by the time we are only ten or eleven years of age. Tragic! Creativity is replaced with compliance and conformity—more so the teachers can manage their classrooms than for the benefit of the children. Follow the rules, stay in line, memorize this, memorize that, repeat what we say, don't be original. When Shawn was in school, at the age of ten, he was told by the teacher that he must use a brown crayon (Burnt Sienna) when coloring a picture of a tree. He could not use a blue crayon! "After all," she said, "trees are not blue!" (Geez.)

Today we live in a post-industrial world that is continuing to change at record pace due to technology at our fingertips, advancements in science and math, and continued changes in global competition. Think about it, for the first time in seventy-five years, we have four generations working side by side in the workplace—Veterans, Baby Boomers, GenXers and GenYers (Millenials). We have entered a new era that many refer to as the Digital Age. Whether you call today the Digital Age or the Information Age, we are living in a time of incredibly complex shifts in culture, technology, lifestyle, communication, and work life. Steven's son is eight years old, he will graduate college in 2026, and he will be at the peak of his income-generating portion of his career in 2048. We have no idea what demands our world will place upon his generation, how different his daily life will be, and what skills and competencies will be required in the workplace.

We wager a friendly bet, however, that our current education system is failing to adapt fast enough to provide the type of learning challenges and experiences that will best prepare today's third graders to enter the workplace in 2026. According to the literature and research we reviewed in brain science, creativity, divergent thinking, psychology, human development, and education, experts far smarter than Shawn or Steven argue convincingly that the need for greater creativity, divergent thinking, critical thinking, and problem solving are critically important to our future success. The 2007 formation of the *National Math and Science Initiative* focused on dramatically improving math and science education in the United States. The work of many organizations, including the Bill and Melinda Gates Foundation, to improve our public school education in the United States is critically important, desperately needed, and greatly appreciated. But we believe there is another crisis in our education system because of the absence of adequate focus on creative thinking in all of its many forms.

We support and encourage all of the brilliant minds working today around the world to further our understanding of the creative process, creative thinking, brain science, and the potential for creativity in our daily lives. In this book we are offering you practical tools and strategies to foster and enable creativity within your daily life at work, home, and at play.

CHALLENGES WE FACE

The challenges to implement a greater focus on creativity in our schools are many and varied in their source and complexity.

This new economy and the world we live in today and in the future require us to produce adults who can think creatively and solve more complex problems than ever before. This is based on the rapid acceleration of technology, cultural diversity from immigration, generational differences in the workplace, global competition, and the massive changes in the nature of work moving forward.

Our education system has been based on feeding workers to the industrial complex for far too long, especially now that we have entered the Information Age. Our entire education system is geared toward college acceptance, yet a college degree today can be worthless as a competitive advantage (just ask the twenty-eight-year-old sleeping in your basement), it's a minimum requirement. Master's degrees are now expected to be competitive in the workplace. Sadly too many colleges today are marginal institutions that are not about academic excellence but rather financial stability. Hence the typical college degree is practically useless and a waste of $100,000 to $250,000.

We have failed to re-engineer our school curriculum from third grade through college, to put creativity, divergent thinking, and creative problem solving as a priority for the new economy. Check out this informative article: http://www.ted.com/talks/ken_robinson_says_schools_kill_creativity.html.

Similar to the poignant message of the film *Faith Like Potatoes*, we must have faith just as a potato farmer that our crop (our future) will prosper from investing in creativity training. Potatoes grow underground; and it is not until harvest time when the soil is dug up and turned over that the farmer discovers whether the potato crop is a prosperous one. Having this blind faith in the power of creativity as a way to prepare our future generations requires leadership, commitment, and consistency over time. This is obviously as hard if not harder as the current struggle to keep music and art classes in our public schools that are plagued by budget cuts, a lack of vision, and a lack of commitment to the value of these educational programs.

One amazing solution for unleashing creativity and innovation to solve problems that change the world is Peter Diamandis' X PRIZE Foundation that provides contests across multiple industries based on Peter's principle of

Revolution through Competition. Creating a 100-mile-per-gallon automobile and developing a manned space travel vehicle are just two examples. One incredible outcome of these X PRIZE contests is the involvement of people who otherwise would have never been involved in these inventions and solutions. School teachers, executive assistants, and high school students, for instance, have participated and some won contests. Check out www.xprize.org and Peter's book, *Abundance.*

THE CHALLENGE TO EMBRACE OUR OWN CREATIVITY

Elizabeth Gilbert, now famed author of *Eat, Pray, Love,* explored the common notion that "Creativity and suffering are somehow inherently linked and artistry in the end will always lead to anguish" in her February 2009 TED Talk, "Your Elusive Creative Genius." Humankind's history of belief about creativity is that it first came from the Greek belief of daemons (mythical beings), and genius seen as a magical divine entity who lives among the creative person, artists, or sculptors for instance, according to the Romans.

However during the Renaissance period, the person and their skills were placed at the center of the creative process. Gilbert aptly said this left us at risk of arrogance and narcissism with the belief that creative people would think "it came from me." This leads to great self-consciousness and possible anxiety and stress once you have made a great creation. Think of all the bands in the 1980s and 1990s that were "one hit wonders," never making another successful chart-topping album or single after the first big hit. Do you remember the song "Billy Don't Be a Hero"? The self-imposed pressure can be immense. Painters unable to lift a paintbrush. Authors staring at a blank page or computer screen for days. Average Joe or Jane Public avoiding the creative process altogether by staying consumed by busy work.

WHY CREATIVITY IS DIFFICULT FOR SOME OF US

Creativity is difficult for some people because:

- It is easier to focus upon what we know how to do in the concrete world, especially when overwhelmed and stressed, so we avoid it.

- It is too difficult to push through the "clear your mind" stage.

- They rush to decision, robbing everyone of quality ideation and assessment.

- They fear making a mistake.

- They fear being wrong. Children are not afraid to be wrong; when they don't know the answer, they try anyway. Steven's eight-year-old son is always coming up with different ideas about the origin of things and why things work the way they do without once ever worrying if it's "wrong" or not. If you are not prepared to be wrong, you will never come up with anything original. Even worse, we stigmatize those who make mistakes at work.

- They fear embarrassment or humiliation from being judged by others.

- Most have been educated out of it by schools, teachers, and sometimes parents.

- Clinical depression makes it difficult for many people to exert any energy toward creative thinking.

- Their addiction to crisis management or "quick fixes" results in avoidance of planning and creative thinking, and staying busy with "busy work."

- Beliefs such as, "Creativity is not productive," keep them blocked from using the creative process.

- They think, "I'm just not a creative person," or "I gave up on being creative a long time ago"—this thinking zaps the energy out of people's creative potential, and may kill it altogether.

- After having a creative success, especially a tremendous success, too often people become consumed with thinking, "How am I going to beat that?"— resulting in creative paralysis.

Elizabeth Gilbert offered a wonderful reframing of our approach to creativity in her 2009 TED Talk when she said:

But maybe it doesn't have to be quite so full of anguish, if you never happened to believe in the first place that the most extraordinary aspects of your being come

49

from you but maybe you just believed they were on loan to you, from some unimaginable source for some exquisite portion of your life to be passed along to someone else when you are finished. This changes everything.

Wayne Dyer says in his new book *Wishes Fulfilled: Mastering the Art of Manifesting,* that he doesn't write his books, instead he writes them by connecting to the "source."

TAKING ACTION DESPITE OUR DIFFICULTIES

Creativity can't happen unless people decide to pursue it. —Robert Sternberg, psychologist

Okay, but don't get down—there is good news. David Kelley, founder of IDEO, a global design consultancy, teaches "creative confidence" at the d.school (Institute of Design) at Stanford University. He believes people fail to pursue creativity because of their lack of creative confidence. Kelley says of teaching creative confidence, "It's to help them rediscover their creative confidence—the natural ability to come up with new ideas and the courage to try them out. We do this by giving them strategies to get past four fears that hold most of us back: fear of the messy unknown, fear of being judged, fear of the first step, and fear of losing control."

The opportunity of creativity is the mix of finding meaningful work and purpose in our lives, with self-expression and procreation, with the massive need to add more value. In this information age, we are now desperate for creative thinkers who can digest and synthesize the mountains of data and experiences made instantly accessible by the Internet, and apply it all to the problems at hand, creating something anew out of the chaos.

Despite a dreadful high school dropout rate of 56 percent and a college acceptance rate of only 30 percent at West Philadelphia High School, the West Philadelphia Auto Academy formed Team EVX to compete in the Automotive X PRIZE. Building a 100-mile-per-gallon (mpg) car created a project-based learning opportunity that provided students with real world experience ranging from engineering to public relations. The group engineered two impressive automobiles, with one achieving 65-mpg capabilities. It was also one of the youngest groups to compete in the global contest. View this video to learn more: https://www.youtube.com/watch?v=8-vqJVJQeNM.

So keep your chin up—there is hope! In the next chapter you will discover that you are creative and have immense power within you to make a difference in this world through creativity. The rest of this book provides practical tools so you can engage and create, so let's get busy.

WORK IT

Make a list of what fears or mental blocks keep you from unleashing your creativity.

_____

_____

_____

_____

_____

_____

Did you have any "Use a brown crayon...trees aren't blue" experiences growing up? Is there an opportunity to shake off these limited thinking experiences?

_____

_____

_____

_____

_____

_____

What are some of the statements or phrases you say that may be shutting down your child's creativity or stifling your co-workers' creativity?

_____

_____

_____

_____

_____

_____

Take a few minutes and think about the potential impact of Elizabeth Gilbert's suggestion to reframe your creative ability as being on loan to you for your use and to then be passed on. Does this free you up to be less anxious about your creative potential?

_____

_____

_____

_____

_____

_____

What are some small or large projects or opportunities in your life right now that you know will benefit by applying your creativity to them?

_____

_____

_____

_____

_____

_____

_____

_____

CHAPTER 3

YOU ARE CREATIVE!

*Everyone is born creative; everyone is given
a box of crayons in kindergarten. Then
when you hit puberty they take the crayons
away and replace them with dry, uninspir-
ing books on algebra, history, etc. Being
suddenly hit years later with the "creative
bug" is just a wee voice telling you, "I'd like
my crayons back, please."*
—HUGH MACLEOD, cartoonist, author of
*Ignore Everybody: and 39 Other Keys to
Creativity*

YES you are creative, and you are not alone. LinkedIn,
with more than 187 million members in December 2012,
announced their Top Ten Most Overused Profile Terms
for 2012, and "creative" is number one for the third year
in a row (United States, Sweden, Singapore, New Zealand,
Netherlands, Germany, Canada, and Australia). I recently
entered a search for "creative" in LinkedIn, and worldwide I
got 3,183,243 profile search results with 1,785,123 of these
in the United States! Don't be bashful, claim your creativity.

We have helped lots of people master their use of LinkedIn—check out www.linkedlaunchpad.com for great free training.

So repeat after us: "I am creative. I am creative."—now click your heels together. We want to help you reconnect to your creativity in all aspects of your life. You are creative, you simply may not think you're creative or realize how creative you are. In this chapter, we are going to continue exploring the reasons you may believe you are not creative and help you understand what you can do to be your "most creative self." If you are a parent, you will also hopefully realize the importance of helping your children maintain their creativity well beyond their tenth birthday.

Here's what we know today about creativity based on brain science, clinical studies, and practical experience throughout the world:

- Creativity is not about IQ or intelligence (95 percent of the world's population IQ is between 70 and 130).

- Creativity is not a talent or special skill that a person either has or doesn't have.

- We all are born with the capability and the potential for creativity.

- We are born as creative organisms.

- "Serious play" is the combination of professional ideation with childlike playfulness that frees us up to be creative for better solutions and innovation.

- Creativity is far too often dismissed as soft and fuzzy and labeled "unproductive time" by many in Western culture, especially in the workplace.

Today our definition of **creativity** *is the process of creating ideas that have value.* **Imagination,** *on the other hand, is the process of bringing to our mind things that are not present to our senses.* **Innovation** *is the process of putting new ideas into practice, or the implementation of creative ideas.*

Creativity is the ability to put yourself and others into a mindset, a way of functioning, which allows your natural creativity to function. In this chapter we are going to show you what must be in place and what you must do in order to enable your greatest creativity, your ability to play. We captured these steps as C.R.E.A.T.E:

Commit with Confidence and Courage

Release Expectations

Embrace Play

Accept

Take time

Engage

Children have no inhibitions when it comes to almost anything, and especially creativity. Children are filled with the wonder of curiosity as a natural state of being. Children embrace their ability to play as a way of life for many reasons—they don't know to do otherwise, they don't judge and criticize the art of play, and children are not hung up like adults are about creativity because they are not afraid to be wrong. Ask a kid, "Who wants to sing?" They all do! One of the biggest blocks to creativity adults experience is their fear of being wrong during the creative process.

Beth Jarmin conducted a study of children and creativity by giving 1,600 five-year-olds a creativity assessment used to measure NASA engineers' creativity. Ninety-eight percent of five-year-olds scored in the highly creative range. Tested again at ten years of age, only 32 percent scored in the highly creative range. By the age of fifteen, only 12 percent scored highly creative. Only 2 percent of adults score in the highly creative range.

The good news is that we are all born with creativity. The bad news is, it gets worked out of us by our current education system, which is a tragedy. While we each may embrace creativity differently, especially in our adult lives, we are all born with creative curiosity, the wonder of possibility, and the openness to play for no other reason than to play.

The great news is all things are not lost for you in terms of creativity. No matter where you are today, or where you believe you are in terms of your ability to be creative, or what your life history is with regard to creativity, there are simple yet powerful techniques and strategies you can use to be the creative person you were born to be.

We know in order to maximize your creativity you must be able to reach an open mindset, which is very difficult today due to our daily information overload and task focus. Joyce Carol Oates, in the *Journal of Joyce Carol Oates 1973–1982*, wrote, "'Keeping busy' is the remedy for all the ills in

America. It's also the means by which the creative impulse is destroyed."

Before we share these strategies with you, let's first check in on one other important factor—the value of being creative in today's society at work and at home. Unfortunately creativity has gotten a bad rap for decades, especially in the workplace. One of Steven's former CEOs with whom he worked for many years used to say things like, "Let me guess, Steven, this is now the time that you're going to do all of that pointy-headed, warm, fuzzy-thinking stuff?" (Sighhhh...) Sadly in this world of being over-scheduled and over-worked, suffering information overload, and what feels like non-stop urgency crisis mode with life balance at risk, it has become far too easy for people to drown in daily to-do lists and dismiss or simply ignore the value of creativity, therefore not making the time or effort to be creative. Ironically, however, when these same people see or experience something creative, they "ooh and aah" with fascination, excitement, and adulation, which is exactly opposite of the criticism they felt for creativity up until that point.

The real value of creativity by definition is the creation of original ideas that add value—value to individuals, teams, customers, the workplace, and sometimes for the greater good or for the well-being of others. Remember some of the greatest inventions in our time were created out of "accidents" from smart, creative people being open to possibility, open to play, pushing the envelope of what is possible. Imagine the world today without Penicillin, microwave ovens, fireworks, Scotchgard protector, Post-it Notes, inkjet printers, X-rays,

Viagra, Rogaine, Corn Flakes, Silly Putty, Play-Doh, Saccharin, and chocolate chip cookies.

Companies such as Pixar, Disney, Apple, Google, 3M, and Zappos are all heralded as creative, innovative market leaders. We have national awards for "Best Company to Work For" and "Most Innovative Company."

The creation of the X PRIZE Foundation "whose mission is to bring about radical breakthroughs for the benefit of humanity, thereby inspiring the formation of new industries and the revitalization of markets that are currently stuck due to existing failures or a commonly held belief that a solution is not possible" is laudable. More than 100 X PRIZE contests have been held to date; and according to their website, "The X PRIZE Foundation is widely recognized as the leader in fostering innovation through incentivized competition." As mentioned previously, Philadelphia high school students built a car that can obtain 65 mpg inspired by competing in an X PRIZE contest.

> The X PRIZE Foundation is accelerating the pace of innovation across sectors ranging from Space exploration to alternative fuels and fostering a clean environment through its various X PRIZE CHALLENGE grants that have energized smart creative teams to come up with breakthrough solutions that have the potential to positively impact the lives of billions of people. —Ram Shriram, Founder of Sherpalo

Think about the different ways creativity pays off in the workplace. The Disney Trading Pins you see Walt Disney World guests wearing on their lanyards have become collectible items; there are annual international conventions where people trade and buy Disney Trading Pins. (Don't tell us that you haven't seen those people walking around at Disney with all their metal!) This idea originated with two hourly paid Disney cast members. Also, flex scheduling and staffing allowing employees to work from home or work four ten-hour shifts instead of five eight-hour shifts, all came out of creative thinking. Finally think of the single parent who works two jobs yet still figures out how to keep three kids fed, clothed, loved, and in school through college graduation.

BECOMING CREATIVE AGAIN—THE C.R.E.A.T.E. PLAN

The following plan will help you set yourself up for success whenever you want to be creative and work through a creative process. This plan is based on expert findings in research and practical application of creativity methods over the years. This is in no way an exhaustive list of every technique, yet we are confident that our C.R.E.A.T.E. Plan represents the most significant issues for setting the stage so that you, or you and your group can be most effective with your creative thinking.

Commit with Confidence and Courage

Release Expectations

Embrace Play

Accept

Take time

Engage

COMMIT WITH CONFIDENCE AND COURAGE

Guillaume Apollinaire (Who? Okay, he is credited with coining the term "surrealism"—or as they call in it in the Midwest, oddball paintings) once wrote, "Come to the edge, He said. They said, We are afraid. Come to the edge, He said. They came. He pushed them and they flew." Truly great creativity requires self-confidence and courage similar to jumping off a cliff. Just as having a parachute helps in this scenario, so too will the C.R.E.A.T.E. Plan help you with your creative process.

Adults' fear of making a mistake or being wrong is a major killer of creativity. You must reframe your creative process as "Whatever happens is okay." Remember the notion of creativity as "serious play."

Some ways to boost your self-confidence and courage in preparation for participating in a creative process are:

- Remember creativity is within all of us; it does not require super intelligence or special powers— you are enough just as you are right now.

- Imagine the benefits and positive outcomes of a successful creative process.

- Ask yourself, *Come on, what's the worst thing that could happen?*

- Realize and remember that stepping away from your work and revisiting it over time allows you to let go of any needs for "perfection in one try."

- Come up with a crystal clear compelling "why" for why you are doing this creative process.

- Ask yourself, *What happens if today's status quo never changes and we do nothing?*

- Remind yourself that creativity is about wonder, possibilities, and opportunity, so stay open to it. Focusing on the right answer or "the" solution shuts you off to the openness needed for creativity to flourish.

- Know yourself—complete the self-assessments in the back of this book, write down your hang-ups or blocking beliefs and attitudes, and identify what you need to do to free yourself.

- Remind yourself of all those great inventions we use today that came as a result of accidents.

- Remember that you are not at the center of creativity, it's not "about you"; instead, it is about you floating on the river and catching what comes to you.

Some examples of how best to get to know yourself in preparation for creativity are:

1. When do you get your best ideas? Night, morning, afternoon? Talking with people? Thinking on your own? Reading or listening to music? Exercising? Outdoors or indoors? Driving? Writing or talking?

2. Are you more visual, tactile, or audible in the way you learn and process ideas? For examples: drawing storyboards or vision boards versus making lists versus journaling versus recording your voice as you talk to yourself or with a group.

Take a moment and write down your thoughts on how to be self-confident and courageous before embarking on your creative process. Self-assessments can be extremely helpful tools to allow you to "see yourself" in terms of your creativity potential. We have provided a list of these in the back of this book in the Creativity Toolbox.

RELEASE EXPECTATIONS

Releasing your expectations frees you up as an adult, allowing you to get more in touch with the creative child inside you. Remember that little person who was tucked away in a closet of your mind so you could focus on your job, car payment, mortgage, the kids, your marriage, volunteering, exercise, and every other task on your to-do list?

Human beings seem to be naturally gifted for passing judgment and criticism. This judgment and criticism kills the creative process. Remember the great question, "Do you want to be right or happy?" Being right or choosing the best solution comes much later in the evaluation stage that Shawn covers later in this book.

Phrases that help you stay open in the creative process and suspend judgment or criticism are:

- What if?

- Imagine if...

- Perhaps we could...

- What do you think if we...

- How would a 6-year-old say it?

- Said a different way would sound like...

- Another way to look at that same thing...

Another expectation you must let go of is expecting the perfect solution in just sixty minutes. A more realistic expectation is to realize that the creativity process will take multiple steps over several days, weeks, or months (depending upon the project) before the best solutions are identified. Therefore, planning enough time for this process ahead of time will alleviate stress and anxiety later.

To truly release your expectations requires you to embrace the possibility of the creative process, respect the time that is involved, all for the purpose of reaching or creating the best ideas with the greatest value.

EMBRACE PLAY

Creativity is not a meeting that you force on groups of employees to "come up with a great idea." To be truly creative and to create the best possible outcome for a group or an individual to be creative, you must create a separate distinct space, we call the Play Zone. The idea is to get away from life, get away from your desk, get away from your daily to-do lists—schedule your time and create a space to quiet your mind. In corporate settings this may only be conference room that is used intermittently.

Before you think creating a Play Zone requires money for a new building or other crazy investments, consider this. Over the past twenty years, Shawn and I have shown people how simply stepping out of their office, returning to their car in the parking lot, turning on the air conditioning or the heater, putting on some music and sitting undisturbed inside their car can become a Play Zone.

However, play zones are not the café at Barnes & Noble, the table in the middle of your employee cafeteria, or your office with the door closed. You have to manage the potential distractions out of your Play Zone. If you work in a corporate office environment, it is best to keep your Play Zone a secret so co-workers don't interrupt you with "Got a minute?" meetings or time wasting "Just dropping by to say hi" conversations.

If you work from home, creating a Play Zone away from your home is incredibly important, unless you are blessed to have a 4,000 square foot home or larger that allows you to sneak to a room far enough away from all potential distractions.

Your Play Zone is also about having a serious play mindset. Some best practices for getting in a creative mindset are:

- Listening to two or three songs or meditating to calm the mind.

- Before entering the Play Zone, make a list of everything you have to do that you are currently worrying about or thinking of, including everything that could interrupt your Play Zone. Making the list (data dumping) seems to free space in your mind allowing you to focus on creativity.

- Take two or three minutes to focus on your goal of the creative process to break your preoccupation on everything else you were doing.

- Your mind will wander when alone, and groups tend to fill the air with idle chit chat. Rather than sit in silence, stay focused in these moments and push through (expect fifteen minutes to be used for transitioning into the creative process).

- In groups, use a hands-on exercise to break the ice. For example, have multiple everyday items on the table in the room and ask participants to make a list of every possible use of the item other than its real purpose.

ACCEPT

To live a creative life, we must lose our fear of being wrong. —Joseph Chilton Pearce

Accept who you are and the people in your group when doing group creativity. Remind yourself that you are "enough," and you bring great value to the process. There is no perfect time and there is no precise moment that you will finally have all of the research, preparation, knowledge, and experience you desire, so stop waiting and dive right in—now. As we shared in the previous chapter about the *Creativity Crisis,* one of the best things you can do to reframe your mindset about your capacity for creativity is to remove your ego from the process by remembering that creativity is a process in which you participate and contribute to, yet from a humble place rather than from an egocentric "it all comes from within me" arrogance.

Remember too that your fear of being wrong is a sure-fire way to kill your creativity. Suspend your need to jump to conclusion or solution. To this end, Sir Anthony Hopkins, while answering questions during his second visit to *Inside the Actor's Studio* (original airdate 10-15-2007), shared the following after discussing the importance of keeping the creative process of acting in perspective relative to the rest of the world, and getting your ego out of your acting so your best work is possible.

> None of this is important. The other cynical thing I will tell you which is shocking. If none of us ever acted again in a film, the world would not come to a stop. If I never went on stage or made a film again. So on. Who cares. And that's a great freedom to know that. I just take it easy and think about what's to be will be. I've got this thing that helps me, Today is the tomorrow I was so worried about yesterday. So

think your best. Unfold. Let go. If you want it, it will happen. Just surrender. Because it has nothing to do with you.

Of course Sir Anthony Hopkins acknowledged this was true before he was a famous actor, as well to counter the criticism that "This was easy for him because he was so successful already," and he emphasized that you must work hard and keep honing your craft, or as Morgan Freeman once said, "You have to keep working, dancing, keep your feet moving."

So remember to release your need for perfection (Release Step), and accept your humanness. Be humble about your approach to the creative process if for no other reason than to reduce your stress or anxiety from any feelings of performance anxiety or negative self-talk.

Be accepting to the potential of the creative process, the fact that it may take a few meetings over time, and the reality that you will never have the perfect team. When working in groups, be sure to touch base with each participant as soon as possible from the beginning and listen for their level of buy-in to the process and its intended outcomes. Listening to yourself and to others is critically important to the Accept Step.

TAKE TIME

Getting started is one of the challenges to having productive and effective creativity time. Too often people tell us, "We don't have time to sit around and be creative." Sadly these folks miss the point altogether. Research and practical experience tells us there is a sweet spot in terms of time dedicated to creativity. Too large a block of time and people won't participate; not enough time and people feel rushed, shortchanged, and become critical of the creativity process or critical of the quality of the outcome.

The best time frame for a Play Zone is sixty to ninety minutes. The next challenge you will face is distractions while trying to focus on your single problem, especially in the first ten to fifteen minutes of the creativity period. When tasked with trying to be creative, either individually or in groups, adults tend to struggle with "not having all the answers" and their need to jump to conclusions or jump too quickly to a solution.

To reawaken your own creativity, you should take time to:

- Read books, magazines, articles

- View videos

- Listen to speeches

- Watch speeches from TED conferences

- Subscribe to creative channels on YouTube such as "Thinkr"

- Enroll yourself in Google alerts for topics you want to follow

- Explore the hundreds of ProjectX contests online

- Sign up for Adult Enrichment classes at your local college

- Research Amazon.com and review recommended book reading lists

- Study improv comedy

- Participate in "open mic night"

- Journal your thoughts

- Doodle or draw

- Paint

- Do yoga

- Ride a bike

- Go for a long walk

Use your DVR or TiVo to record television shows such as:

- *Whose Line is it Anyway?*

- *Drew Carrey's Improv-aganza*

- *How Things are Made*

- *Invention Hunter*

- *Shark Tank*

- *CSI*

- *House*

- *Breaking Bad*

- *Big Bang Theory*

- *America's Got Talent*

- *Chopped*

- *CashCab*

- *Million Dollar Remodel*

- *How Do They Do It?*

- *How the Universe Works*

- *Invention*

- *MythBusters*

- *Pitchman*

- *Why Didn't I Think of That?*

Research these shows on Hulu.com, Netflix, Amazon Prime, or VideoOnDemand.

Engage all of your senses. Squeeze clay between your fingers. Try cooking a new recipe. Listen to your favorite music; change your radio preset stations in your car every other week for variety. Play with Legos. Look at websites of companies that are heralded as creative—Apple, Zappos, Legos, Whole Foods, Salesforce.com, Amazon, Tencent Holdings, Natura Cosmeticos, Reckitt Benckiser Group, Ecolab, Activision Blizzard, Pixar, Proctor & Gamble, L'Oreal, Schlumberger, Alcon, NetApp, Juniper Networks, and Chipotle, to name just a few.

Check out blog sites:

- Blog.creativethink.com

- AccidentalCreative.com

- IdeasonIdeas.com
- 99u.com
- CreativeSomething.net
- CreativeGeneralist.com
- Idea-sandbox.com/blog
- blog.guykawasaki.com
- 52Projects.com
- InnovationManagement.se
- Gapingvoid.com

Download apps on creativity:

- Creative Whack Pack
- Dr. Babb's Idea Lab
- Brushes
- Paper
- Bebot
- WriteRoom
- Whrrl
- Artnear
- Postino
- iTalkRecorder

Look up Pinterest pinboards. Check out Digg, Reddit, and LinkedIn news. Kickstarter.com has hundreds of projects. Check out Kiva.org. Read Bill Clinton's book, *Giving*, which lists hundreds of nonprofit organizations and causes around the world. Read Dave Lakhani's *Power of an Hour*. Visit TimFerris.com for inspiration, intrigue, and innovation. Go to www.creativitylaunchpad.com to take your creativity to a whole new level.

ENGAGE

Commit to tolerating the discomfort and the ambiguity of the creative process longer to create the best ideas and solutions and to leverage opportunities. Commit to take action, no matter how small or big. Be present, especially when working within a small group. And finally, focus on the outcomes, the results, and the benefits of persevering through the creative process.

C.R.E.A.T.E. PLAN

Now identify the problem, desired outcome, or challenge statement with which you want to apply the C.R.E.A.T.E. Plan. Take a few minutes to complete this plan so you can move forward in powerful, positive ways with your creative process. Under each section, simply write down the specific, timely actions you must take to achieve success in your creative process.

My Goal Statement (desired outcome or challenge). (For example, solve the clean water shortage in Sub-Saharan Africa.)

_____

_____

_____

_____

Commit with Confidence and Courage

_____

_____

_____

_____

Release Expectations

_____

_____

_____

_____

Embrace Play

_____

_____

_____

_____

_____

Accept

_____

_____

_____

_____

Take time

_____

_____

_____

_____

_____

Engage

_____

_____

_____

_____

_____

The first five things I must do to set myself up for success are:

1. _____

   _____

2. _____

   _____

3. _____

   _____

4. _____

   _____

5. _____

   _____

I commit to myself that I will use the C.R.E.A.T.E. Plan to prepare for my next creative process on or before _____ (Date MM/DD/YYYY).

You may also download this plan at www.creativity launchpad.com/jumpstart.

WORK IT

Take time to think about each aspect of your life that would benefit greatly when you apply a little creative thinking to it.

_____

_____

_____

_____

_____

What specifically would be the value or benefit to you and/or other important relationships in your life from applying a little creative thinking?

_____

_____

_____

_____

Which of these are urgent AND important enough to start working on right away? How will your life be different if you simply focus a little time, effort, and creativity in this area of your life?

_____

_____

_____

_____

_____

What specifically do you have to do or what thinking do you have to change to truly release expectations for the best outcomes of your creative process?

_____

_____

_____

_____

_____

_____

What specifically do you have to do to create the time and space for creative thinking? Alone? When doing this with a group of people? What resources and support do you need to protect this time and space?

_____

_____

_____

_____

_____

Make a list of all of the benefits of letting go and accepting the imperfection of the creative process. If I just let go I would...

_____

_____

_____

_____

_____

_____

INDIVIDUAL CREATIVITY

*My future starts when I wake up every
morning. Every day I find something creative to do with my life.*
—MILES DAVIS

IN this chapter we give you some ideas, strategies, and tools
for developing your own individual creativity. As we have
pointed out in previous chapters, you already have the ability
to be creative; in fact, we believe you have the ability to be a
creative genius because you were born with it! Now the idea is
to take your creativity, wake it up, slap it around, shake it up,
and put it to good use.

The first question you have to ask yourself is, "How do I
spur my own creativity?" Think of creativity as a magnificent
horse. You are using your spurs to motivate it to higher levels
of performance. A spur is a pointed device secured to a rider's
heel used to urge on the horse. We want you to urge on your
creativity stallion!

How? Let's explore some of the techniques you can experi-
ment with to discover what your specific spurs are for kicking

your creativity into high gear. For example, one of the activities that inspires Shawn and stimulates his creativity is visiting art museums. Another element is being able to talk to a very creative and innovative person and bounce ideas off of that person. Steven loves attending conferences and participating in webinars where people are talking about new strategies and unique ideas. He also enjoys reading articles in magazines or on websites that have unique approaches to something that greatly spurs his creativity. The key is to find out what it is for you, and there is no one, right answer because the answer is different for each person.

There is a well-known story about Edwin Land, who one day was walking with his daughter in the woods. He took a picture of his daughter with his camera and his daughter then said, "Daddy, can I see the picture you just took of me?" He patiently explained to his daughter that she could not see the picture right away; she had to wait for it to be developed. As a child she did not understand why she had to wait and found the idea to be somewhat ridiculous. This got Land thinking, "Why can't a picture be seen right away? Why do we have to wait to see a picture?" He immediately began working on what would eventually become the world-famous Polaroid Instant camera, released in 1948. The spur for his individual creativity was words from a child. The spark or the stimulation can come from any source. (Incredibly, sixty-one years later, in 2009, Polaroid announced their new Z2300 Instant Camera that prints a 2" x 3" smudge-proof, tear-proof, full color photo print.)

The question you need to ask yourself is (after careful observation), "Both in the past and in the present, what are items, events, or processes that stimulate and spur my individual creativity?" For some people it may be gardening. For others, it may be cycling. And for others, it may be watching an old movie or walking along a river or swimming in the ocean. Notice when you feel you are being your most creative and look back to see what it is you're doing at the time. Then of course the idea is to recreate that circumstance as much as possible.

Make a list of things you feel spur your creativity and try to do them more and surround yourself with those kind of materials and experiences. The key is to be conscious of what makes you creative. We find in our speaking and training programs that a lot of people can be creative, but they don't know in which circumstances they are the most creative. You need to find out what it is. Now.

FOSTERING YOUR CREATIVITY

In addition to finding out what your creativity spurs are, you need to work on and foster your creativity. We find the most creative people are people who continue to develop and foster their creativity throughout their entire lives. They just never stop.

How do you foster your creativity? We believe there are several techniques for fostering and improving your level of creativity. Here are some ideas (wow, can you imagine in a book about creativity we're going to give you ideas?):

Fitness

No this is not a misprint! We're sure the last thing you expected to find in a book about creativity is a mention of fitness and health. We know that people who are more fit and eat a healthier diet have a tendency to be more creative. Why? The main reason is they have more energy, they think more clearly, and as everyone knows, when you work out many helpful chemicals (endorphins, serotonin, dopamine, and BDNF) are released into your brain. The number of positive emotional effects gained from regular exercise is surprising. These effects include improved self-esteem, enhanced mood, better memory and mental functioning, and decreased stress. The decrease in depression is significant, as depression is one of the mental blocks to accessing your creativity. If you want to be more creative, a regular routine of fitness can enable you to stimulate your creativity to higher levels.

Reading

There are four forms of reading that can dramatically improve your level of creativity. The first form of reading is reading books (physical or electronic) that contain how-to techniques. These books give you models, tools, and techniques to create ideas and evaluate them. This book you are reading right now is an example of a how-to book. The second form of reading is to read books about creative people. For example, you could read a book about Steve Jobs, Gustave Eiffel, Thomas Edison, Mary Kay, Picasso, or Dolly Parton— any person who is considered highly creative. The advantage of reading biographies about highly creative people is you can learn from their life experiences and liberally steal their techniques for coming up with ideas. The third form of reading is to read any books at all whether they are fiction or nonfiction. The idea here is that when you're reading your thinking is stimulated generally, and can often lead to great ideas, which are unrelated to what you're reading specifically, but your mind was stimulated somehow. We are often shocked by the number of people we meet in society who never read. We don't say this as a form of judgment, but we do believe those people are limiting their creativity. The fourth type of reading is not in book form, but reading online articles, websites, or electronic versions of magazines. Because the Internet is in real time, there is often more current information online. For example, Seth Godin, the marketing genius, posts a daily blog. Check it out at www.sethgodin.com. Go to your nearest bookstore and wander through the magazine racks. Check out the article titles for inspiration.

Training

There are many organizations (both for-profit and non-profit) that have internal training departments. Many more organizations are now offering programs on creative and critical thinking to their employees. In the single or multiple-day creativity programs we offer, most people find them to be extremely valuable because they learn techniques they never knew for developing ideas and evaluating ideas. Contact people in your Training or Human Resources Department to find out if this kind of training is offered. If this kind of training is not offered in your organization, don't let this stop you. Invest your own money in seeking training on how to be more creative and innovative. Yes it will cost you money on the front end, but you will recoup your money by being more creative and innovative.

Training programs are most likely available through your local colleges and universities or through training companies that travel around the country with open enrollment courses. Additionally, there are many online resources for learning about and fostering your creativity. One example is our product called *Creativity Launchpad,* which you can see by visiting www.creativitylaunchpad.com. If your current company does not offer it for you, then do it for yourself. It is an investment in your future.

Videos

Practically any topic you want to learn is available in a video format somewhere, someplace, somehow. Do some research online and locate DVDs or downloads you can tap into online. One example of this is Ted. What is Ted? Ted is a conference held across the country where highly creative experts get on stage and deliver fascinating keynote presentations about different topics. Ted's tagline is "Ideas worth spreading." One quick glance at the Ted website, at www.Ted .com, gives you thousands of videos to look at—and they're all free. Free you say? Boy, that's a shock! It's not a shock in the world of the Internet. If you want to learn to be more creative and you want to foster your creativity and study creativity, simply go online and look for video clips about creativity. There are tons of them.

We often get calls from people who want to be professional speakers. We are willing to spend about half an hour with someone on the phone who wants to be a professional speaker. Here however is the big issue—during our discussion we ask them if they have read any books about professional speaking. They answer "No." We ask if they have watched any videos about professional speaking. They answer "No." We then ask if they have read any articles about professional speaking. They answer "No." At this point we're more than a little frustrated with the person who has not sought out any of the resources available at their fingertips.

Just by pressing a few buttons, you can learn a great deal by tapping into the web. Take advantage of it!

Mentors

People go to a gym and work with a personal trainer. They take lessons from a golf coach to be a better golfer or from a tennis coach to be a better tennis player. Yet we find most people do not think of the idea of having a mentor for creativity. Obviously the old saying holds, "Two heads are better than one." Think of all the people who are in your life, and on that list think of the top three creative people who you know personally or professionally. Ask one of them to be your creativity mentor. The idea behind a creativity mentor is not to only have someone to brainstorm with and run creative ideas by, but to have someone who can teach you more about creativity. Just make sure your creativity mentor is someone who is more creative than you are and who has a track record of being creative. Then set up some sort of process when they can mentor you over a certain period of time. It may be three months or six months, and you may meet with him or her about once a month—but set up a structured process. And yes, in case you're wondering—you can learn to be better in terms of creativity.

Coaching

There are many professional coaches in the marketplace who do executive coaching, motivational coaching, time management coaching, financial coaching, and even grief coaching. Seek out, find, and hire a professional coach who can coach you on creativity and innovation and critical thinking. Yes there is an investment required on your part, but we guarantee it will pay off. If you're going to learn, then learn from the best.

Projects

Both of us have often found that being involved with significant challenging projects at work results in modest and major breakthroughs in terms of our individual creativity. At one company Shawn worked for, the company was planning for a national meeting and it was suggested having a company history museum display. Rather than running in the other direction from the project, Shawn thought it would be fun and challenging, so he volunteered for the task. Over a two-month period he had to curate, assemble, and build a company history museum that could be transported to the site of the national meeting. It turned out to be a big hit. Many people saw rare items in the museum and learned a lot they did not know about the company's early days. But don't miss the key point, by participating in the creation of the museum, Shawn was able to apply all of his creative talents in project management, influence, negotiation, graphics, visual elements, and design.

One challenge with the museum project was to create an entrance to the museum that blocked people's view from seeing what was inside, yet was fully portable and could be set up in a hotel ballroom. This of course was all done on an extremely limited budget. Shawn was able to create an eye-catching museum entrance completely built from lightweight foam core material, which was colorful and cut into shapes to look extremely modern and aesthetically pleasing. By volunteering to participate in a project at work, you can learn how to apply your creative skills and abilities, and more importantly enhance them. You also learn you have the ability to be creative and have more talent than you realize. Check out www.strengthsfinder.com to learn about your strengths so you can choose projects that tap into your strengths.

Nonprofit Work

Another way to foster your creativity is to do work with charitable, nonprofit organizations. By working with teams of people to help the charity, you will be forced to come up with creative ideas and solutions in order to help the organization achieve its goals. Because nonprofits often lack money and resources, you're often forced to be much more creative than you would be normally. This gives you the ability to learn how to solve problems in different ways and to learn from other people who are working with your team and how they solve problems.

Action Planning

Once you have completed this chapter on individual creativity, pull out a piece of paper and create an action plan for your individual creativity development. This plan would include what you're going to do in the next three to six months to enhance and foster your creative abilities individually. The plan needs to include three basic elements: 1) what you're going to do, 2) how you're going to do them, 3) a timeline or measurement for each item. For example, on your list you might write, "I am going to read one book on creativity." Next, write the title of the book, and next to that write the specific date you plan to finish reading the book. This really is like having a workout plan at the gym; this is a workout plan for your creativity!

Environment

Put either one of us in an empty room with blank walls, and we have the ability to be creative. Put either one of us in a room with flip charts, markers, music, and props, and then put this room on Walt Disney World property—and we will be much more creative. Don't underestimate the value of an environment that stimulates your creativity. We were once presenting a creativity and critical thinking program in Pennsylvania at an insurance company. On each table in the room we placed odd items. On one table there were two or three strange items such as a whisk broom, a box of 20 Mule Team

Borax, a sculpture of a fish, and a giant fishing lure. It was so interesting to see the expression on people's faces when they walked in and sat down. Before the training started, we could see the energy level go up as they were looking at the odd mix of items on the tables. We did this technique on purpose to illustrate the environment definitely can be stimulating for creativity, or it can be a creativity killer. From an individual creativity perspective, we want you to look at four areas that are important in your environment: your office, your home, your car, and your network.

Your Office

We realize that most organizations have specific rules and regulations as to what is allowed in an office space. At the same time we also realize there are several elements within your control. If your office or cube space is an area where you will be participating in work that requires creativity, why not give yourself an advantage by having a creative office space? By now you probably know what stimulates your creativity. It may be certain books, it may be flowers and plants, pictures on the walls, or a set of rotating screen savers with different images. Try to figure out which elements you need to have in your office to help you be more creative. These elements can be broken down into several different categories:

- *visual* - pictures, calendars, flowers, small sculptures, collectibles, candles, screensavers

- *auditory* - music, a small fountain, a white noise machine

- *texture* - fabrics, wood, desktop surfaces

- *scent* - cologne or perfume, incense, flowers, air fresheners, candles

- *touch* - stress balls, desktop play toys, rubber bands

- *taste* - candy, gum, mints, nuts, popcorn

The big idea is to have a creative space that stimulates as many senses as possible. Try to create a space where you are incorporating some of the elements from each category, and you'll find your creativity will be dramatically enhanced. Steven has an 18-inch sculpture of Pinocchio and Jiminy Cricket on his desk, Mickey Mouse on his bookshelf, and a bag of marbles he rolls around in his hands whenever he is thinking. Later in this book you will discover some great tools that you should have near your desk at all times as well.

Your Home

We believe your home should be your castle, your oasis, your place to get away from the world at large and be at your best. Take a closer look at your home and see if there is one room or one area that could be your creativity area—home office, "man cave," covered corner on your backyard deck, or even a converted closet, for example, where you can create the perfect environment with no restrictions except your own. Shawn is in the process of dividing his home office in half. It is a large space with an open floor plan. Half of the office will be an art studio and the other half will be a functional office.

This is designed to make his office creatively stimulating as much as possible.

Your Car

We're sure listing the car is somewhat of a surprise to you as a reader; however, many people spend a lot of time in their car every day. We know many people who commute a total of at least two hours or more each day in their car. What if your car could be stimulating in terms of creativity? How is that possible? Using a little creativity, of course. Here are a few ideas for making your car more creative:

- *No Radio.* Don't just listen to the radio, have specific downloaded music or audio CDs you find most inspirational and stimulating, or change your radio's preset stations every few months to expose yourself to new ideas and perspectives.

- *Rolling University.* Back in the old days, salespeople used to call their cars a "Rolling University" because they would listen to instructional or motivational audios whenever they were driving around in their sales territory. Take the same idea and purchase several audio programs on creativity and innovation (how-to and biographies). Each day on the way from work or to work listen to them. You will be learning and getting creative stimulation while you drive!

- *Call People.* Use the time in your car to call people and brainstorm with them on the phone while you're driving—hands free, of course!

- *Quiet Time.* When you have a specific problem or challenge, reserve quiet time in your car on the way to work or on the way home to think it through. Turn off the radio or the CD and just quietly reflect on the problem with no interruptions, and don't answer the phone—you are in the "Do Not Disturb" mode.

The same ideas apply if you ride a train or bus every day. Use your time wisely! Now your car or train becomes a source of transportation *and* a source of inspiration!

Your Network

In Shawn's book *Jumpstart Your Motivation*, he covers the value of surrounding yourself with the right people as part of your social network in order to enhance your level of motivation. He also mentions the idea of eliminating negative toxic people who will destroy your level of motivation. We believe the same applies in some ways to creativity. If you associate with people who are not creative, who are negative and not open to new creative and innovative ideas, it will negatively impact your ability to be creative. The idea, as far as your network goes, is simple. Hanging out with more creative people enables and inspires you to become more creative. Creative people try to hang around with other creative people, which enables them to become more creative. Carefully review all of your friends and acquaintances, spend a little less time with those who are less creative and more time with those who are more creative.

Please take the time to sit down and take a hard look at every element of your environment and what you can do to adapt or change it in order to be a more creative person. You'll be glad you did—and your creative brain will thank you.

WORK IT

What kind of training could you get to help with your creativity?

_____

_____

_____

_____

_____

_____

Who could be your potential creativity mentors?

_____

_____

_____

_____

_____

_____

Where could the creativity area be in your home?

_____

_____

_____

_____

_____

_____

How could you change your car time to be more creative?

_____

_____

_____

_____

_____

_____

Who should you add to your network?

_____

_____

_____

_____

_____

_____

CHAPTER 5

GROUP AND ORGANIZATIONAL CREATIVITY

...1,541 CEOs and senior leaders cite "creativity" as the most important leadership quality for business success in the next five years.
—IBM GLOBAL CEO STUDY,
"CAPITALIZING ON COMPLEXITY," 2010

IN 2010, more than 60 percent of the CEOs interviewed in IBM's Global CEO Study believed industry transformation was the top factor contributing to uncertainty. This same study found "the biggest challenge facing enterprises from here on will be the accelerating complexity and the velocity of a world that is operating as a massively interconnected system." What the heck does that all mean? It means in plain English, to quote Bob Dylan, "the times they are a-changin'."

In this chapter we offer our list of leadership principles and practices to help you lead and enable your people to harness their creativity in the face of uncertainty and constant change...our new "normal." Don't worry, you are completely normal if you just saw yourself wrangling cats in a rainstorm (really you are...). Everyone today is doing more with less! You will also learn our "3D" approach to meetings, especially meetings with creative groups or projects requiring creativity and creative problem solving. We wrap up this chapter with tips on how to best reward or inspire your group to embrace and engage in the creative process.

Before you lead any group in a creative process, you must understand what ingredients are necessary to improve creativity, especially in business settings. The following are offered for your consideration:

- *Expertise*—including technical, organizational, procedural, operational, and intellectual knowledge with adequate viewpoints and perspectives represented

- *Trust and Safety*—healthy, effective, productive, positive team who genuinely wants the best for their fellow team members, values each other and cares enough to look out for one another consistently

- *Creative Thinking Skills*—open to possibilities, flexible, imaginative, divergent, and convergent thinking

- *Context*—clear understanding of the scope of the problem or opportunity, its history, "Why now?," why it is important to the organization, group or individuals, and the value a solution brings to the organization, its people and/or the people it serves

- *Motivation*—external factors and internal drivers to motivate and engage are keys for success, especially in terms of long-term buy-in and lasting motivation

- *Time Commitment*—serious understanding and support of the time required of participants to achieve meaningful, productive, profitable results

- *Value Appreciation*—genuine acknowledgment, acceptance, and appreciation for the results, outcomes, or value achieved as a result of the creative process...not lip service, but truly valuing the work, results, and their impact

Take a moment to think about each of these factors and how they are reflected within your current group or organization.

Shawn's book, *Jumpstart Your Motivation*, provides several powerful strategies for maintaining your motivation. To encourage and enable motivation within your group, be sure to focus on the following:

- Fit—right role for the right person at the right time

- Freedom—the autonomy for people to achieve the goals

- Resources—having the tools required to get the job done

- Team—support, caring, flexibility, trustworthiness, and recognize talents

- Encouragement—acknowledgment, praise, and positive challenging

- Organizational Support—collaboration, info sharing, communication

Now let's take a look at the leadership principles and practices that enable groups to be more creative. We offer you this list based on mountains of well-known research studies, surveys, and years and years of our own practical experience training leaders and team members alike.

A creative leader...

- adjusts to the winds of change with grace and flexibility.

- approaches strategy and planning frequently, nimble to adapt.

- listens to employees, partners, and customers to create great value.

- encourages the sharing of ideas among everyone, equally.

- embraces disruptive innovation and ambiguity that may linger.

- listens, decides, tests and tweaks, decides and corrects quickly.

- allows "failing fast and often" to discover the best solution.

- has the courage to challenge status quo in a healthy way.

- will adapt, invent, and create as a way of life.

- expects the future to be drastically different.

- loves to ask why, see the possibilities, yet take real action now.

- encourages confidence in creativity and a willingness to take risks.

- focuses on mastery and excellence.

The leadership lessons we have learned from the past twelve years of "Happiness Research" also help a leader more fully engage their team members in the creative process. Basically the four fundamental components of happiness for a person are: 1) self-perceived control of life, 2) self-perceived progress in life, 3) the quality of personal connections, and 4) the extent to which a person feels part of something bigger than him or herself with meaning and purpose well beyond surviving daily life. Most people want to know what they do matters.

Interestingly, much of what a creative leader practices positively contributes directly to "self-perceived control" and "self-perceived progress," while also impacting the quality of one's connections and the amount of meaningful work and purpose.

OUR 3D MEETING PROCESS

In Chapter 7, we offer several *Process Tools* that help individuals and groups manage their creative process. Our 3D Meeting Process is perfect right now as we discuss managing your creative process with groups. Basically this 3D Meeting Process came about, created by Steven, when he was consulting for healthcare companies and hospitals. His clients' biggest complaint was the dysfunction and time wasting of group meetings, especially project team meetings.

The most common reasons team meetings are so dreadfully painful or mind-numbing to attend are (aside from the fact they are boring!) (in no particular order):

- No agendas or ineffective agendas

- Poor use of time to discuss any issues in depth

- Involving too many people who otherwise could be doing something else

- No ownership of next steps or accountability to handle issues, and report back to the group in the future

- Avoiding, sometimes completely, the "real issues at hand"

- Practically never making a decision

- Booking way too many "bad" meetings

The 3D Meeting Process improves your meeting process, especially for creative projects, in many ways:

- Your meeting process has a distinct beginning, middle, and end

- Meetings can be far shorter in length (15-30 minutes)

- Participants tend to focus with far less distractions

- Meeting attendance is higher for lots of reasons

- More people become genuinely involved in the process and care more about the outcomes

- Often better decisions are made with far greater buy-in (novel thought, ay?)

- The success experienced by the team enables momentum and buy-in for future 3D Meetings (people want to come to your meetings—that's cool!)

The 3D Meeting Process consists of three distinct separate meetings that are always conducted in the order of *discovery,* then *distribution,* and finally, *decision.* Here's the 3D Meeting Process in a nutshell:

Discovery

The first meeting solicits feedback from all participants; for example, brainstorming all the possible reasons xyz problem is happening at work. In Chapter 7, we share our proven technique, *Idea Webbing*, which enables you to collect lots of information from your group quickly yet still collect it in an organized way that allows participants to take ownership of a specific topic, research it, and bring their findings to the next meeting. For example, the group is deciding whether or not to buy a pet dog for their team office, and using *Idea Webbing*, the group identifies the following topics that require further research—cost of a backyard fence, whether the office complex allows dogs, the best breed of dog to buy, comparable information for cats instead of dogs, grooming requirements, where to keep the dog when no one is in the office for extended periods of time, and so on. Basically once the brainstorming through *Idea Webbing* is done, the group would ask for individuals in the group to choose a topic they are willing to enthusiastically and adequately research and study in order to make a recommendation to the group at the next meeting, the Distribution meeting.

Distribution

The Distribution meeting has a laser-focused agenda, which is for each person or team of people who agreed to research an item during the Discovery process, to report their findings orally to the entire meeting group. All meeting participants are instructed to take detailed notes as they listen to each "report out." The facilitator of this meeting makes sure everyone is clear about the information that was shared, hosts a brief Q&A session for clarification purposes, and then instructs the group further. The facilitator asks each individual participant (or group) to turn in a written/typed copy of the list of their findings. After the meeting, the facilitator can email to everyone the detailed notes from the discussion if a scribe captured the notes during the individual reports and/or use the list of items collected from each individual or group. Typically these meetings are scheduled one week apart, sometimes two weeks apart. The homework assignment for all attendees is to consider all of the information received during the presentations, because they will be asked to make a recommendation based on all of the presentations at the next meeting, the Decision meeting.

Decision

This final meeting is the opportunity for the group to reconvene, allow anyone to either present their information again, or provide new information gathered since the previous Distribution meeting. Using any one of a number of strategies for the group to decide on their final selections, the facilitator guides the group through a final decision-making round. The group then either concludes the meeting and a separate meeting to plan the execution of these decisions is held at a later date; or, the group conducts a final piece of business at the end of this Decision meeting, which is to strategize the execution plan, and then move forward from there.

If your group is much like the groups we have worked with in the past, don't be surprised when participants "can't believe how productive these meetings were" and how shocked they are "this group made those types of decisions." The positive experience from this 3D Meeting Process should obviously be leveraged to continue forward progress with your group(s).

Feeling good about the meeting and decision-making process is great. Building momentum for more positive embrace of future meetings should naturally occur. But you may find your group still has people who need to be incentivized for engaging in creativity or creative projects, or your entire group wishes to be incentivized. Unfortunate but true. Sure it would be great if everybody just contributed because it was the right thing to do; but reality says, we will need some form of incentives for some groups. Let's take a look at what works and why.

CREATIVITY INCENTIVES

We could spend the next 400 pages discussing the science, art, psychology, and legal aspects of employee incentives, so why don't you get comfortable, pour yourself a drink, pull up a blanket, and stay a while. No doubt you have more important things to do than read 400 pages, so we'll give you the most important tips you need to know. Ready?

As a college intern in the Disney College Program at the Walt Disney World Company, Steven worked as a front desk host at the front desk of the Grand Floridian Beach Resort. He fell in love with the hotel business and thought he had found his "perfect career." One day his manager told him the company was offering a contest to all Cast Members (employees) at the Grand Floridian, to name one of the grand suites in the resort. The prize was something like dinner in the employee cafeteria and $100 cash. Steven read all the instructions, and he studied the theme of the hotel and the idea behind the suite. Remember, Disney is huge about theming. Over the next week or so, he did his research at the local library, studied the décor and the names of the other suites on property, and spent hours thinking about the name for this new suite.

Two weeks later, at an employee meeting, the general manager announced the winner of the "Name the Suite" contest, "Congratulations go to Steven Rowell!" He was elated. To this day Steven can't remember what he ate in the cafeteria and he doesn't remember what he spent the $100 on either. The million dollar question of course is, "Why did Steven spend all that time and money to research the project?" Now think about some of the many possibilities for responses Steven could choose, "I need the $100," "It's a fun contest," "I want to impress my parents and my girlfriend," and so on. Truth be told, Steven was willing to spend so much time on the contest because he knew the name would be on that suite forever and it was a great legacy memory from his college internship.

True story—and the grand suite is still named and themed exactly how Steven had designed it twenty-three years ago! Steven has told that story to whoever will listen, over and over again. The secret these companies—those voted "Best Company to Work For" or "Most Innovative Company" or otherwise have dominated their industries—know is that employees want to contribute in meaningful, lasting ways and simply be recognized for it. Believe it or not, it's not about money or gift certificates or Employee of the Month parking spaces. Frankly, the best companies have figured out it isn't about money at all, most of the time. It's about recognition.

As you think about your own organization, your own group and its culture, and what you think your people would want, consider the following list of ways to incentivize people to creatively engage at work, school, or volunteering:

- Announcement in the company newsletter

- Meet n' Greet with the CEO

- Coffee and a Donut with _____

- Part-time opportunity to work with the XYZ division, department, or team

- Lateral job transfer to a new division/department

- Promotion

- Current job changing to incorporate more of the skill area involved in the contest

- Lapel pin worn every day

- Headshot photo posted on a Celebration Wall

- Name listed in the credits of a movie (like Disney listing on the movie credits, the names of babies born during the production of a Disney Animated Feature)

- Name on a plaque forever

- Scholarship or giveaway named after the person

- Name a sandwich in the employee cafeteria after the person

- Winner gets to record the company phone greeting

- Take part in "Bring Your Dog to Work Day"

These are creative and fun. You get the idea. Yet there is another aspect of incentivizing team members to be creative, especially when it is for contribution to a project or simply going above and beyond the call of duty in terms of creativity or engagement. Think about my buddies who were animators and artists at Walt Disney Pictures/Pixar. Or a group of customer service associates at Wegman's grocery store. Flight attendants on Virgin Airlines. Or nurses in a children's hospital.

The leadership keys to remember when inspiring or even incentivizing team members are:

- Pay attention, listen, observe, and catch them in the act—be present

- Respond quickly, immediately if possible—the worst is to receive a note card in the mail at home six weeks later with a computerized signature

- On the other hand, a handwritten note mailed to their home within forty-eight hours could be one of the most memorable gifts you can give

- Document the performance and memorialize the behaviors—no one has ever said the boss celebrated their hard work too much

- Allow people take on junior leadership or point person roles as part of their career advancement—this one is huge and commonly used in creative jobs like animation, theme parks, and hospitality/tourism careers

- Quality time spent with people who they admire and respect is powerful—coffee with the CEO is just one example

- Have them interact with your customers in a fun, unique way to celebrate

- Invite them participate in committees, task forces, training teams, or other unique opportunities

- Name a fun award after them

- Be consistent, fair, and timely in response and in treatment of all recipients

- Ask them what they would like to celebrate (novel, I know...seriously?)

In the next chapter, Shawn is going to share with you some of the best models you can use right away to be more creative. In fact, he will show you our incredibly powerful and helpful RD² Creativity Tool.

WORK IT

Reflecting upon the list of ingredients necessary to improve creativity, especially in business, which one is missing and therefore you need to improve?

_____

_____

_____

_____

_____

What do you need to stay motivated? What do you think your team members need to stay motivated?

_____

_____

_____

_____

_____

_____

Review the list describing a creative leader and identify which behaviors you are already doing consistently, and
which ones you could improve.

_____

_____

_____

_____

_____

_____

Which of the creative incentives will you implement in
the next thirty to sixty days?

_____

_____

_____

_____

_____

_____

What would happen if you started meeting with your team members individually and simply ask them what they want and need?

_____

_____

_____

_____

_____

_____

_____

_____

CHAPTER 6

MODELS FOR CREATIVE THINKING

Our Age of Anxiety is, in great part, the
result of trying to do today's job with yester-
day's tools and yesterday's concepts.
—MARSHALL MCLUHAN

MANY people believe in order to be creative you have to start completely from scratch. The reality and one secret to being creative is to use systems and processes that people before you have created to help you think differently about a situation, problem, or challenge. In our work as consultants and trainers, we find that a lot of folks have never heard about some of the famous creativity models that already exist. First, let's talk about how we define a model (and we are not talking about the ladies on the Price is Right!). A model is simply a system or a process someone has already developed and used as part of the creative thinking process. The purpose of this chapter is to give you some models you can use when you are stifled or trying to come up with creative solutions to a problem, opportunity, or challenge. So try them, you might like them.

When we work with groups on creative and critical thinking programs, often people are skeptical about following a model to be creative. They say that following a step-by-step process will not help their creativity and would stifle their creativity. This is not true; the reality is by walking their problem, opportunity, or challenge through different models, we have found they come up with better and different answers. After people work through the models we teach, they end up saying things like, "It really forced us to think about that in a different way." or "We came up with solutions we would not have come up with otherwise." They are surprised at how effective the models are.

Before we get into the specific models, the following are a few general guidelines for using them:

- *Don't discount a model or a process before you use it.* You really don't know how it's going to work until you try using it. Keep in mind these models have been proven by thousands of users over many years.

- *Don't use models on problems that are extremely simple.* Generally speaking, most of these models for creative thinking are designed for more complex in-depth problems or issues.

- *Don't fall in love with one model and use that one all the time.* Use different models in different circumstances.

- *Make sure you understand in-depth how each model works before you use it.* We recommend reading the materials prior to using them with a group.

We thought we would start out by giving you our model we developed called the RD². (It stands for Rowell–Doyle squared.)

RD²

Some general rules about the RD² model:

- Have fun.

- Be crazy and silly.

- Be messy.

- Be illogical.

- There are no limitations.

- There is no judgment in the early phases.

- There are no wrong answers.

- Items can be added to the list at any time during steps one through seven.

- Even if you're in step seven and you're picking the final solution, if a new solution pops into your head, you are allowed to add it.

- The ideas must be displayed so all parties can read them.

- You must have a certain period of time of uninterrupted thinking time to be as effective as possible (1 to 2 hours).

- Save all of the paper to refer to later. For more information about how to use the RD^2 Model, visit www.creativity-launchpad.com/rd2.

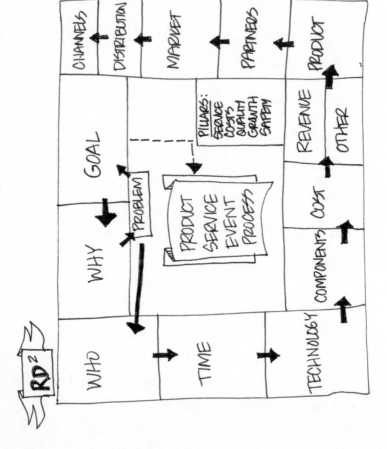

The following are some other models you may have heard of that have been fairly successful in terms of generating creative ideas or thinking differently:

SIX THINKING HATS (TM)

The six thinking hats model was developed by Edward de Bono. Edward de Bono is a Maltese physician, author, and consultant who is the originator of the term, *lateral* thinking. His book *Six Thinking Hats* is a perennial favorite and best-selling classic popular in schools and universities to teach people how to think through a problem, situation, or challenge in a different way, utilizing six different types of thinking for individuals, groups, or team processes.

The main idea behind six thinking hats is the human brain thinks in a number of distinct ways and each of these ways can be challenged. De Bono thought there should be a structured way to develop tactics or processes for thinking about a problem. He wanted to remove the randomness of the thinking process. The concept behind the six thinking hats is to think about a problem from the perspective (filter) of a particular hat color. Thinking in each of the six hats, the brain will identify and bring to mind certain aspects of issues being considered. In essence, it forces people to think about a problem in a different way from how they probably would otherwise. The six thinking hats are described by de Bono as follows:

White Hat

This is the "information hat" or as people often describe it, the doctor hat, where you're considering what information is available, "just the facts," with no emotions involved whatsoever—this is the purely objective viewpoint.

Red Hat

This is the one that operates from intuition or instinct involving emotions and feelings but not particularly with any specific justification.

Black Hat

This could be considered the hat of the pessimist, focused on all the reasons why a solution will not work and should not work, and the logic applied to why the organization should be both cautious and conservative toward the solution.

Yellow Hat

This is described as the "hat of harmony," and considers the logic identified with the benefits of the solution and the positive upsides to this potential solution.

Green Hat

This is thought of as the "magic hat" and how we can make it work using statements of provocation and investigation, and seeing where the thinking goes in evaluating all of the possibilities.

Blue Hat

This is the hat that always finishes the discussion. This is the "hat of the facilitator" who then clarifies the who, what, where, and when. As for the solutions, the blue hat evaluates the outcomes of the thinking and what should be done next.

We have seen de Bono's hats used in many different ways. As an example, when a group forms to consider a problem, opportunity, or challenge, you would ask each person in the group to adopt the perspective of a certain hat color. Some people bring the specific colored hats to a meeting for everyone to wear. "Owning" a certain hat forces the wearer to think about a problem in a different way. If a person is normally an optimist who thinks about all the reasons why something should work, then having them wear the black hat to identify all the reasons why something won't work can lead to new ways of thinking and possibly identify issues otherwise missed by the group. We often hear people say thinking of a problem or situation from this perspective is extremely helpful.

Here is a variation of the six thinking hats model, which can be very effective. When thinking through an issue and evaluating with a group, you can ask different people to assume hats for various departments. We call these functional hats. Even though clearly they are not part of the department, we get together in our group and for example say, "Let's look at this issue from the perspective of sales, marketing, accounting, legal, human resources, manufacturing, and shipping." Individuals in the group would then each assume the perspective of the sales hat, the marketing hat, etc. The six thinking hats model forces you to think from a different viewpoint.

OSBORN-PARNES MODEL (OP)

Alex Osborn was one of the partners and founders of BBDO advertising. In the 1950s he became fascinated with the process of creativity and wanted to know if the creative process could be labeled and organized into a step-by-step model. He consulted with Dr. Parnes at the University of Buffalo and together they created the Osborn-Parnes Model of Creative Problem Solving (CPS). This model is complex and designed to look at a problem in a different way, and most people in our creativity programs find the process to be extremely valuable. The only objection some people have with the Osborn-Parnes (OP) model is that it is time consuming. Once you've used the process a few times, it does not take nearly as long. The argument in support of OP is that taking the time to identify the real problem before you work on it saves you time on the back end. Far too many times people try to solve problems before they know with any certainty what the real problem is. This model is public domain and can be used by anyone. The model is designed to generate many different ideas through brainstorming and to deliberately defer judgment in order to critically evaluate possibilities and ideas.

Definitions

Before giving you the steps of the OP model, it's important to understand how they define certain terms. *Creative* is an idea that has an element of newness or uniqueness, or at least the one who creates a solution and also has value and relevancy. *Problem* is any situation that presents a challenge, opportunity, or a concern.

The Six OP Steps

1. *Mess Finding*—An effort to identify a situation that presents a challenge

2. *Data Finding*—An effort to identify all known facts related to the situation to seek out and identify information not known but essential to the situation

3. *Problem Finding*—An effort to identify all the possible problem statements and isolate the most important underlying problem

4. *Idea Finding*—An effort to identify as many solutions to the problem statement as possible

5. *Solution Finding*—Using a list of selected criteria to choose the best solutions for action

6. *Acceptance Finding*—Making every effort to gain acceptance for the solution to determine a plan of action and implement the solution

One of the most important aspects of the OP model is to be patient and not skip steps in the process. Additionally, the OP model uses both divergent thinking (meaning lots of possible solutions) as well as convergent thinking (meaning narrowing down the possibilities). Now let's take a look at each step in detail.

Step One: Mess Finding

The first step in the OP model is to discover what the problem may be. Write a list of several statements relating to the topic that begin with "I wish," "I want," and "It would be great if...." Next, evaluate your list and decide which items you, a) are most bothered by, b) have the most influence over,

c) are willing to work on. Once this list is worked through, then make a list of "I wishes."

Step Two: Data Finding

After you've narrowed down your thoughts in Step One and have your list of "I wishes...," select one "I wish..." statement that you want to work on through Step Two. Notice, we still have not identified the problem specifically. Now ask yourself multiple questions about your "I wish..." statement:

- What resources do I have?

- Who can help me?

- How did the situation occur?

- What will happen if I don't do anything?

- Why is this important to me?

- Why can't I just do nothing?

- What are the benefits of a solution?

- What are the drawbacks of a solution?

- What other information do I need?

- Has this problem/situation occurred before?

- When does it bother me most?

- When does it bother me least?

Some of the answers may make sense and be relevant and some may not, but we still have not identified the problem.

Step Three: Problem

There are three techniques used in Step Three to find out more about the problem. The techniques are 1) "Five Whys" 2) In what way might I...? 3) Keywords. In the "Five Whys," keep asking "why" to determine your true motivation for your initial wish.

Someone says:

"I want a new house." Why?

"Because I need a larger house." Why?

"Because I like to have big dinner parties and invite all my friends." Why?

"Because right now my house is kind of embarrassing because it's too small." Why?

"Because status and image are very important to me." Why?

So the "Five Whys" help you get to the root cause of the issue, or awfully close.

"In what way might I..." is used to keep you from boxing yourself into a corner. You make a statement, and then change one word in the statement to see if you can change the question because the answers also change. For example:

- In what way might I *generate* more revenue?

- In what way might I *create* more revenue?

- In what way might I *build* long-term revenue?

- In what way might I *create other sources* of revenue?

- In what way might I *find* more revenue?

- In what way might I *borrow* more revenue?

- In what way might I *need less* revenue?

Step Four: Idea Generation

In this part of the process, simply use different creative brainstorming techniques to come up with potential solutions. Please see Chapters 1 and 7 for additional ways to generate solutions. Be sure to download our RD^2 Ideation tool from our Creativity Toolbox.

Step Five: Solution Finding

This is the step in which you will judge the quality of the ideas generated and select the best ideas based on specific criteria and standards. Please see Chapter 8 for an explanation of criteria charts and weighted criteria charts.

Step Six: Acceptance Finding

This is the final phase of the process where we have moved past defining the problem and finding solutions and on to the rest of the process. First, envision the project as complete; second, evaluate a list of events needed to complete the project, plan events, and figure out how to sell the idea to others. Think of this as the marketing phase of the OP model.

The OP model can be extremely helpful in evaluating complex problems, issues, and challenges; people in our training programs have found the process to be extremely valuable.

These are some models you may want to consider using in your specific situations to solve problems, generate new ideas, or address challenges in a unique fashion. As Shawn's father often says, "It's not the job, but having the right tools." These models are powerful tools.

One caution: We are not suggesting you use these techniques without reading about them further, so we strongly recommend that you read more about the RD^2 model by visiting our site at: www.ultimatelaunchpad.com. We believe exposure to these models will help you begin to understand there are hundreds of models out there relating to creativity and innovation that can be used to stimulate and motivate you to higher levels of creativity and better ways of generating ideas.

WORK IT

What creative thinking tools have you used in the past?

_____

_____

_____

_____

_____ __

Looking at guidelines for using models, which ones do you sometimes *not* follow?

_____

_____

_____

_____

When and where do you think you would use the RD^2 model?

_____

_____

_____

_____

_____

_____

When and where do you think you would use the OP model?

_____

_____

_____

_____

_____

When and where do you think you would use the Six Thinking Hats model?

_____

_____

_____

_____

_____

CHAPTER 7

PROCESS TOOLS

*We cannot solve our problems with the
same thinking we used when we
created them.*
—ALBERT EINSTEIN

SIMILAR to the people in Chapter 6 who say "models of creativity" stifle their creativity, you may be thinking, *Process Tools? Eeeekkkk! I don't want to do a bunch of Six Sigma Quality Improvement fishbone diagrams and Pareto Charts!* We hear you and we definitely understand your concern. Our goal for you with this chapter is to share some of the process tools we have found to be helpful as part of the creative process. Again, there are hundreds of models available, many that blur the lines between types of creative thinking, problem solving, and decision making. We are focusing here on tools to help with the creative process.

Picture yourself walking toward a brand new grocery store that you have never seen. Now I meet you at the front door, and I take you on a quick tour of the grocery store, pointing out the layout and explaining the basics of each section.

"Here's the deli where they cut meat to your order, this is the seafood counter where you pick up fresh seafood including live lobsters, and over here is the bakery where all the fresh breads are baked daily. You'll find milk and juice in aisles 4 and 5," and so on. Similar to this brief grocery store tour, we are going to take a tour of some process tools. You may choose not to use all of these tools and that's okay. We want you to know what is available to you.

In this chapter we highlight Framing Tools, Business Process Mapping, Cause Effect Diagrams and Sample Causes, Idea Webbing, and Creative Problem Solving processes.

FRAMING TOOLS

The discomfort some people suffer with the ambiguity of the creative process comes from the lack of context, historical reference point, or simply a lack of a "conceptual anchor" when they approach the creative process. Framing or reframing helps you put your problem or opportunity in a context to which you can relate. Framing is a form of data gathering or uncovering, sometimes done as a series of questions or through a guided discussion. The framing tools we will share are Five Ws, Pillars, SWOT, Mad-Glad-Sad & Stop-Start-Continue, and "If you could change…."

Five Ws

The Five Ws are questions, and the answers are considered basic information gathering. They are a solid beginning formula for trying to capture "the whole story." The Five Ws are:

- Who is it about?

- What happened?

- When did it take place?

- Where did it take place?

- Why did it happen?

- How did it happen? (bonus question)

Each question should have a factual answer, not simply yes or no.

The Pillars

Reflecting upon Jim Collins' books *Good to Great* and *Built to Last*, the quality of decisions made by executive teams at companies Collins studied were found to be far better when as many of the "pillars" as possible could be incorporated into the decision-making process. The pillars were identified as service, quality, cost, growth, and people. Since 1999, some companies have added pillars such as safety, efficiency, and productivity. The most successful companies in Collins' research made executive decisions based on two or three pillars, whereas less successful companies often made decisions based on only one pillar. Sadly, too often that one pillar was cost.

Creativity, the generation of original ideas that add value, impacts all of the pillars. Creativity impacts productivity, product and service offerings, quality of work life, profitability, expanding markets, and simply better ways to do things than are being done today. The reason we include this tool here is that it prompts you to think about a variety of great topics that all need to be covered. When you are brainstorming or idea webbing, you can jog your memory with the list of pillars to make sure you are covering everything. We use the pillars as a memory jog in our RD² process as well.

SWOT Analysis

First of all this has nothing to do with police work! That is SWAT. This is SWOT. SWOT analysis is a structured planning method used to evaluate the Strengths, Weaknesses, Opportunities, and Threats involved in a project or in a business venture. A SWOT analysis can be carried out for a product, place, or person. Setting the objective should be done after the SWOT analysis has been performed. Strengths are the characteristics that give it an advantage over others. Weaknesses are characteristics that place the team at a disadvantage compared to others. Opportunities are things that the project could exploit to its advantage. Threats are items or issues in the environment that could cause trouble for the business or the project. Once gathered, the information can be used to determine if the objective is attainable; if not attainable, a different objective must be selected and the process repeated. The items identified during the SWOT analysis, similar to the pillars, provide more important information that will be extremely important at the evaluation step of the creative process.

Mad-Glad-Sad & Stop-Start-Continue

Mad-Glad-Sad & Stop-Start-Continue is Steven's proven feedback solicitation process that is outlined in detail in

Steven's book, *Success from the Inside Out*. A skilled facilitator can simply collect the information for this process from a group of employees or team members, identifying which comments are the most common among the entire group and what issues need to be addressed first. The first half of the survey process deals with the question, "What are you mad about, glad about, and sad about working here?" Or it could be, "What are you mad about, glad about, and sad about in terms of how we take care of our customers?"

The second half of the survey process deals with the question, "What should we stop doing, start doing, or continue doing to take better care of our customers?" You can replace the "about working here?" or the "how we take care of our customers?" with any piece of information you want to learn from this group of people. After all the data is collected, themes are identified, allowing the management team or project team to process the data and look for trends, opportunities, and solutions.

"If you could change any one thing immediately about..."

If you could change any one thing immediately about how we take care of our customers, with no limit on resources to make it happen, what would you change? Again, you would change the wording of the question to fit your need.

BUSINESS PROCESS MAPPING

Business process mapping refers to functions involved in defining exactly what a business does, who is responsible, to what standard a process should be completed, and how the success of a business process can be measured. Once this is done, there can be no uncertainty as to the requirements of every internal business process. The main purpose behind business process mapping is to assist organizations in becoming more efficient. A clear and detailed business process map or illustration allows outside firms to come in and look at whether or not improvements can be made to the current process.

The four big steps of process mapping:

1. Process identification—gaining a full understanding of all the steps of a process

2. Information gathering—identifying objectives, risks, and key controls in a process

3. Interviewing and mapping—the point of view of individuals and designing actual maps

4. Analysis—utilizing tools to make the process run more effectively

ISHIKAWA DIAGRAMS

Ishikawa diagrams, also called fishbone diagrams, herringbone diagrams, cause-and-effect diagrams, or Fishikawa are causal diagrams created by Kaoru Ishikawa (1968) that show the causes of a specific event. Common uses of the Ishikawa diagram are product design and quality defect prevention, to identify potential factors causing an overall effect. Causes are usually grouped into major categories to identify these sources of variation. The categories typically include:

People: Anyone involved with the process

Methods: How the process is performed and the specific requirements for doing it

Machines: Any equipment, computers, tools, etc. required to accomplish the job

Materials: Raw materials, parts, pens, paper, etc. used to produce the final product

Measurements: Data generated from the process that are used to evaluate quality

Environment: Conditions—location, time, temperature, and culture in which the process operates

Causes in the diagram are often categorized, such as the 6 Ms in manufacturing, 7 Ps of marketing, or the 5 Ss of the service industry.

IDEA WEBBING

As mentioned in Chapter 5, *Idea Webbing* enables you to collect lots of information from your group quickly yet collect it in an organized way so participants can take ownership of a specific topic, research it, and bring their findings to the next meeting. In Chapter 5, the example was a group deciding whether or not to buy a pet dog for the office. First the group identified the following topics that required further research—cost of a backyard fence, whether the office complex allows dogs, the best breed of dog to buy, comparable information for cats instead of dogs, grooming requirements, where to keep the dog when no one is in the office for extended periods of time, and so on. After the brainstorming is completed, individuals chose a topic they were willing to enthusiastically research and study to made recommendations to the group at the next meeting.

An example of idea webbing follows:

- Mom and Dad to purchase a dog.

- Do we buy a dog?

- All ideas

- Sub ideas related to one idea in bulleted list under main idea

- Color changes

- Connecting them makes the webbing

- Best for teams to divvy up the responsibilities

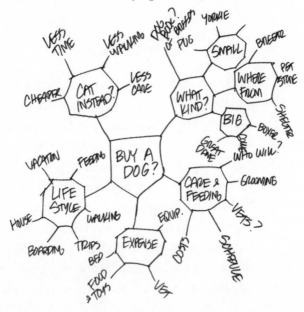

NAKAMATSU CREATIVITY PROCESS

Just for fun...Yoshiro Nakamatsu, also known as Dr. NakaMats, is a Japanese inventor who has become something of a minor celebrity for his inventions. He is a prolific inventor, reportedly having over 4,000 patents, although the confirmed number of inventions is in question. In his interviews, Nakamatsu described his "creativity process," which includes listening to music and concludes with diving underwater, where he says he comes up with his best ideas and records them while underwater. He also built a million dollar toilet room made completely out of gold that he claims helps make him think better. Nakamatsu also has an elevator in his house that he claims helps him think better. He strictly denies that it is an elevator, but rather a "vertical moving room." Nakamatsu's goal is to live at least 144 years—he is 84 years of age in 2013.

Whether you use formal process tools, modify an existing one for your own use, or simply do as Nakamatsu apparently has done and create your own processes from scratch, commit to creating your own process and take the time to enjoy the journey.

WORK IT

When do you think you would use the five whys?

_____

_____

_____

_____

Which process tools have you not used? Why?

_____

_____

_____

_____

Which one have you used?

_____

_____

_____

_____

_____

When could you use process mapping?

_____

_____

_____

_____

_____

_____

Which tools are you excited to try?

_____

_____

_____

_____

_____

_____

CHAPTER 8

CREATE AND THEN EVALUATE

It is not the facts which guide the conduct of
men, but their opinions about facts; which
may be entirely wrong. We can only make
them right by discussion.
—NORMAN ANGELL

WE were working with a company's marketing group in South Florida. The goal was to come up with as many marketing ideas as possible in one day. Using various brainstorming techniques and tools we provided, the group came up with fifty flip chart pages of ideas in eight hours. On each flip chart were ten or eleven ideas, which meant there were over 500 ideas. The group leader turned to us and said, "Well it's great we now have 500 ideas...but what now?"

We patiently explained the goal was to evaluate each of the ideas, but not on the same day. Our philosophy is: "You create, then you evaluate." These two processes ideally should not be done on the same day or at the same time. They are two separate processes. The create phase is for creating without judgment, and the evaluation phase is the exact opposite, to evaluate and judge.

In this chapter we give you tools and techniques for evaluating ideas. In our training and development practices we often see groups who are completely puzzled about how they should evaluate ideas. They ask questions such as:

- How do we tell a good idea from a bad idea?

- Is it just based on a gut feeling?

- How are good ideas measured?

- Aren't good ideas qualitative and not quantitative?

- How do we explain how we selected ideas to our bosses?

- How do we justify our selections?

- How do we explain our selection of ideas from a business perspective?

- What would be potential metrics?

These are all legitimate and reasonable questions. If you're involved with a business, a nonprofit organization, or an educational institution, you know the importance of sound business decision making.

You need to first identify how you're going to measure ideas in terms of criteria and metrics, and then use the proper tools to filter ideas through specific filtering processes. Criteria are simply the facts you're going to use to evaluate an idea. We even like to refer to criteria as business criteria. For example if you are looking at a potential solution to increase sales, you could use some of the sample criteria below as filters to analyze that idea:

- increase profits

- increase revenue

- increase efficiency

- reduce labor

- increase of speed

- increase productivity

- reduce waste

- eliminate redundancy

Okay, you get the idea. Business criteria should be things that if you talk to your executive board about, they would be pleased and would find the criteria relevant to the business. Unfortunately, many times we meet people who say they want to act on an idea because it is cool or hip or neat or cutting-edge. Based on our experience, most people in the executive suite don't want to hear about cool or hip or cutting-edge. They want to know directly how an idea is going to impact the metrics of the business.

So what we need to do then is build a list of metrics that we are going to use to evaluate and measure the business relevance of an idea. This will give you and your team a tremendous amount of credibility and weight when having discussions about ideas and solutions with anyone, including your CEO.

When we have developed a list of criteria, then we need to figure out measurements for those criteria. For example, if you say increase speed, you need to say increase the speed on what and by how much. In a manufacturing plant, you might say to increase the manufacturing line speed for product X by 2 percent in the next thirty days. If you can then tie a dollar amount to the increase in speed, all the better.

After we have developed a list of criteria and we have figured out measurements for those criteria, we are then ready to evaluate the ideas that were developed during brainstorming or ideation sessions. How? There are some simple tools for evaluation and there are some complex tools for evaluation.

If you have people in your organization who are certified in Six Sigma, they will be very familiar with some of these tools. Some of the tools have a tendency to be more objective and some of the tools have a tendency to be more subjective. Please be aware that no matter what evaluation tool you use, there will always be some level of subjective thinking involved, because people always have opinions that sway their decision making.

POLLING

Polling is one of the simplest methods of evaluating ideas in a group. The first version of polling is to present ideas on a chart and have people simply vote on their favorite. The second version of polling is to give each person in the room three sticky dots, and then each person goes up to the charts and puts their dots on their top choices. They can either put three dots on three ideas or all of their dots on one. At the end of that exercise simply count up which ideas have the most dots.

Obviously there are some advantages to polling. It is quick, simple, and easily done. However, there are some significant disadvantages:

- When explaining to others how the selection was made, saying, "We took a vote." has less credibility.

- Polling really does not consider specific criteria when people are analyzing an idea.

- Group Think Risk—peer pressure can convince people to change their vote when they start to see where the dots are. If they're one of the last people voting, they could possibly change their vote based on how everyone else voted.

BEN FRANKLIN CHART

The Ben Franklin list is often described as a plus and minus list. Yes, this list technique was invented by Ben himself. You simply draw a line down the middle of a piece of paper or a flip chart page. On one side, at the top of the page, is a positive sign and at the top on the other side is a negative sign. You make one list for each idea; so if you had six ideas, you have six charts. Once you have completed six charts you then count which idea had the most positives and which idea had the least negatives. By subtracting the number of negatives from the number of positives, one idea for one chart will end up having the highest score. This is the one that will be selected.

The advantages of the Ben Franklin chart are:

- It is fairly quick yet a little more specific on each idea.

- You have more credible information for explaining why you made the selections in terms of the positives and negatives for each of them.

The disadvantages of the Ben Franklin are:

- You still have not applied a specific criteria or measurement in evaluating an idea or solution.

- It is incredibly subjective.

CRITERIA CHART

The Criteria Chart, although it seems complex, is simple to use. On the left-hand side of the page on a flip chart, you write all of the ideas. As an example, if there are six ideas, you write down six numbers down the left-hand side of the page. On the top of the criteria chart you draw columns, and each of those columns will contain a specific criteria such as reduce labor, increase sales, increase profit, etc. One key as you're developing the Criteria Chart is you must get agreement from each person in the room as to the criteria people will agree upon. Be willing to invest some time and critical thinking about the criteria you use, especially the definitions and descriptions of each criterion.

Once everyone in the room agrees on the six to seven criteria that should be written at the top of the page, you are then ready to get feedback on the individual ideas. Using a Likert scale of one to five, with one being the worst and five being the best, you ask the group about idea number one, "How do you rank this idea as it relates to reduced labor?" You get agreement from the group on a number on a scale of 1 to 5; write the number on the chart. This process continues for idea number one all the way across the seven columns. After going through the same process for all of the ideas, add up the numbers across so that each idea has an overall number score. Of course the idea with the highest number is the one that wins.

There are several advantages to a Criteria Chart:

- It is more objective, eliminating some subjectivity.

- It is more criteria based.

- It is more credible as you can explain how you arrived at your answers.

- It forces people to look at an idea from a criteria standpoint.

There are some disadvantages to a Criteria Chart:

- It is sometimes hard for people to decide on a number from one to five.

- The criteria for the number is too often not clear.

- Even after the process some people are still not satisfied with the answer.

- Too often it is missing measurement (i.e., increase sales).

MEASURED CRITERIA CHART

A measured criteria chart works exactly the same way as a Criteria Chart—the only difference is the criteria will be measured. So instead of writing at the top of the chart increase sales, it will say increase sales by 2 percent in quarter one. The advantage of having a Measured Criteria Chart is the criteria is more specific and clear.

WEIGHTED CRITERIA CHART

A Weighted Criteria Chart works exactly the same way as a regular Criteria Chart and a Measured Criteria Chart. The significant difference on a Weighted Criteria Chart is each of the criteria now have a weight. Often executives will say, "Well some criteria are more important than others," which can be true in some cases. The idea behind a Weighted Criteria Chart is to take each criterion and decide the percentage importance of each. For example, you might say profitability is 60 percent, and increase sales is 20 percent, and so on. You follow the exact same process you do for a Criteria Chart where numbers are assigned to each idea. The only difference is that criteria are then multiplied times the percentage to get a final number. This approach gives credence to some criteria being more important than others.

So those are some ways to evaluate ideas that can be extremely valuable and helps eliminate subjectivity.

CRITERIA CHART

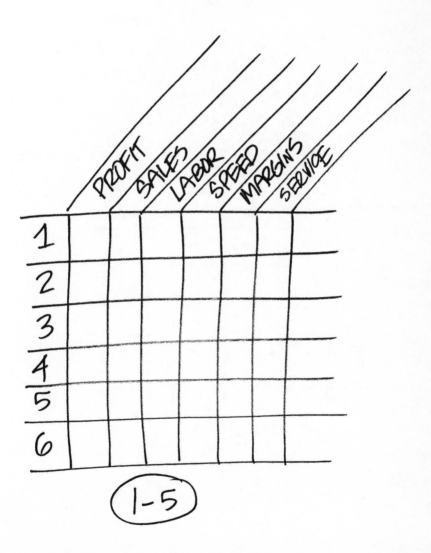

MEASURED CRITERIA CHART

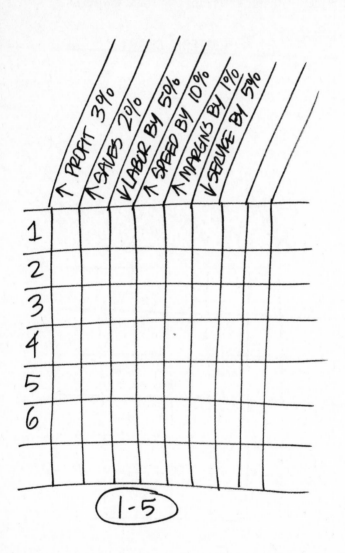

WEIGHTED CRITERIA CHART

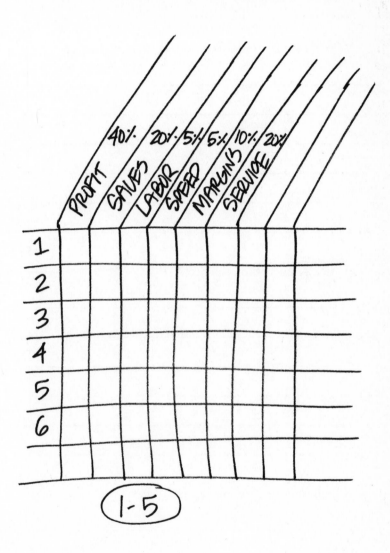

WORK IT

Which evaluation tools have you used in the past?

_____

_____

_____

_____

_____

_____

Which ones worked the best?

_____

_____

_____

_____

_____

Which ones worked the least?

_____

_____

_____

_____

_____

_____

_____

Which process tool listed in the chapter seems to be most relevant to your team?

_____

_____

_____

_____

_____

Why would they be important?

_____

_____

_____

_____

_____

_____

CHAPTER 9

CREATIVITY IN ACTION

Whatever creativity is, it is in part a solution to a problem.
—Brian Aldiss

CONGRATULATIONS on reading this far! Did you know 91 percent of all books purchased are never read according to the Association of American Publishers? We present this chapter as an inspiration to all of our readers as we celebrate people and organizations who have lived with abundant creativity and created true innovations, leaving this planet better than it was before.

We hope you will read this chapter with an open heart and mind allowing you to be inspired by an idea, technology, process, product, or system. Please be sure to visit www .creativitylaunchpad.com to see the most up-to-date celebration of creativity and innovation. We know the following list is in no way exhaustive or far reaching in terms of industries and types of examples. We are sharing what we found to be true innovators either creating something out of nothing, or creating a wholly new product, resource, or service that fills a real need.

HOUSE OF CARDS ON NETFLIX

The first "television show" produced for Netflix members only. Congratulations to the producers who had the courage and vision to adapt to the digital age. Possibly as cataclysmic as the disruption of music CDs going the way of 99 cent downloads on iTunes, we may see this new combination of broadcast media and the digital age flourish creating an entirely new platform or distribution channel for creative digital content.

LIFESAVER SYSTEMS

Making filthy water drinkable for 65 cents? Incredibly inspiring global solution. Visit:
http://www.ted.com/talks/michael_pritchard _invents_a_water_filter.html and
www.lifesaversystems.com.

DIGITAL DETOX TRAVEL ADVENTURES

The latest attempt at helping people globally break their addiction to their technology devices, Digital Detox vacations allow people to attend a "dude ranch" type experience with no television, no Internet connection, no cell phones, no alarm clocks or watches, and no video games. The American Psychological Association has officially termed the addiction "Internet Use Disorder" and will list it in their Diagnostic and Statistical Manual of Mental Disorders for 2013. The Digital Detox retreat co-created by Levi Felix and Brooke Dean: thedigitaldetox.org. Also visit: whyy.org/cms/justyouwait/2013/01/05/hello-world/.

SIERRA LEONE YOUTH

Tapping into the Minds of Sierra Leone Youth—be inspired by what one child did with transistor radios and other modest electronics. Follow his story as he traveled to America and served in a fellowship at MIT as a fourteen-year-old boy. Visit http://www.crowdrise.com/innovatesalone.

This is a donation site, but in no way is a donation expected or encouraged. We simply share the story with you.

TABASCO SAUCE

The urban legend/parable about how to increase sales of McIllhenny Company's Tabasco Sauce is a great mind tingler. As the parable goes, after hundreds of hours working on a solution including business plans, ad campaigns, and marketing initiatives, a college intern sitting in a meeting said, "Why don't you make the hole bigger?" She meant simply drill the hole at the top of the bottle larger so more sauce would come out when the consumer used Tabasco. While this story is a myth, McIllhenny Company nonetheless credits this story as a valuable parable about innovative thinking on their website.

CROWDFUNDING

No longer does the high school rock band member have to wonder from where the money for his next guitar picks or drumsticks will come. Crowdfunding to the rescue! Kickstarter, the leader in this space, is a funding platform for creative projects. Microlending meets social media—crowdfunding has given even a one dollar donor an opportunity to make people's dreams come true. Crowdfunding sites include:

- www.kickstarter.com

- www.crowdcube.com

- www.indiegogo.com

- www.luckyant.com

- www.demohour.com

- www.idea.me

- www.gambitious.com

- www.Rockthepost.com

- www.zaozao.com

- www.rockethub.com

- www.fundable.com

- www.togather.asia

- www.ziibra.com

BETABRAND

Creators of the secret wedding dress, elope dress, and gluttony pants, which expand three sizes larger (sizes: Piglet, Sow, Boar), this whacky group also came up with Sock Insurance; for $13 a year, they will send you single socks once a month. Visit www.betabrand.com.

RECYCLED WEDDING DRESSES

Recycling meets consignment shop for wedding gowns. Check out this novel concept that has people fighting both sides of the coin on this one. Side One—never do it in a million years, disgusting; Side Two—wow, what a great idea especially in this economy. Visit www.preownedweddingdresses.com and www.recycled bride.com.

24-HOUR-A-DAY DONE-FOR-YOU LAUNDRY AND DRY CLEANING

24-hour fitness gym meets local dry cleaners. This new concept has launched with rave reviews—we list it as an innovation to an otherwise 100-year old commodity service, your laundry. Visit www.dashlocker.com.

TSA SNEAK-A-PEEK

Arguably despised by more people than the Postal Service and the IRS, TSA (Transportation Security

Administration) has started posting a weekly sneak peek at the items they are finding in airports during security scans. Visit www.blog.tsa.gov.

ZAPPOS.COM

Tony Hsieh, Zappos CEO, decided, with the help of survey expert Gallup, to offer new hires $1,000 to quit the company after completing thirty days of employment. Tony's hunch, which turned out to be right, incent people to leave and when they turn down the money, their loyalty to their employer vastly increases. Gallup proved Tony right, and allegedly he now offers new hires $2,000 to quit. Reportedly less than 2 percent of all offers are taken by employees who average an income of $11 per hour.

NO MORE WALLET

Check out Square.com and Paypal for innovative new ways to pay at the cash register without using your debit card or credit card. Scary? Or brilliant? Both?

For more fun examples of creativity and innovation, visit www.creativitylaunchpad.com.

APPENDIX A

CREATIVITY TOOLBOX: RESOURCES*

For more creativity resources, updated frequently, please check out www.creativitylaunchpad.com/toolbox.

SELF-ASSESSMENTS

The following self-assessments, some directly related to creativity and others in support of creativity, are available online.

CREAX Creativity Self-Assessment: www.csa.creax.com

Creative Bits Self-Assessment:

http://creativebits.org/ego/creativity_self_assessment

Creativity Habits:

www.creativity-portal.com/articles/edward-glassman/
  assess-your-creativity-habits.html

Host of surveys:

  http://www.indiana.edu/~bobweb/Handout/d8.khatena.htm

including:

- Khatena-Torrance Creative Perception Inventory
- Gough Personality Scale
- Creativity Behavior Inventory
- Creative Attitude Survey
- Runco Ideational Scale (RIBS)
- NEO-PI-R

ASSESSMENTS IN SUPPORT OF CREATIVITY

Learning Tactics Inventory—identify your preferred learning behavior:

http://www.ccl.org/leadership/assessments/LTIOverview.aspx

Behavioral Styles: www.platinumrule.com

Strengthsfinder 2.0: www.strengthsfinder.com

Brain Training: www.lumosity.com

BOOKS THAT INSPIRE YOU TO BE CREATIVE EVERY DAY

Whole Mind, Daniel Pink

Out of Our Minds: Learning to be Creative, Ken Robinson

Creatively Ever After: A Path to Innovation, Alicia Arnold

Think Better: An Innovator's Guide to Productive Thinking, Tim Hurson

The 4-Hour Workweek, Tim Ferris

Cracking Creativity: The Secrets of Creative Genius, Michael Michalko

Creativity Workout: 62 Exercises to Unlock Your Most Creative Ideas, Edward de Bono

Thinkertoys: A Handbook of Creative-Thinking Techniques, Michael Michalko

Thinkpak, Michael Michalko

Admired: 21 Ways to Double Your Value, Mark C. Thompson and Bonita S. Thompson

Abundance, Peter Diamandis and Steven Kotler

Millionaire Messenger, Brendon Burchard

Giving, Bill Clinton

Freakonomics and Super Freakonomics, Steven D. Levitt and Stephen J. Dubner

Blink and Outliers, Malcolm Gladwell

VIDEO LINKS

http://www.ted.com/talks/ken_robinson_says_schools
_kill_creativity.html; 2006
http://www.ted.com/talks/sir_ken_robinson_bring_on
_the_revolution.html; May 2010
http://www.ted.com/talks/ken_robinson_changing
_education_paradigms.html; Oct 2010

BLOG SITES

- www.Blog.creativethink.com

- www.AccidentalCreative.com

- www.IdeasonIdeas.com

- www.99u.com

- www.CreativeSomething.net

- www.creativity-online.com

- www.CreativeSomething.net

- www.CreativeGeneralist.com

- www.Idea-sandbox.com/blog/

- www.blog.guykawasaki.com

- www.52Projects.com

- www.InnovationManagement.se

- www.Gapingvoid.com

APPS ON CREATIVITY

- Creative Whack Pack

- Dr. Babb's Idea Lab

- Brushes

- Paper

- Bebot

- WriteRoom

- Whrrl

- Artnear

- Postino

- iTalkRecorder

*We provide no endorsement, claims, or otherwise to the quality of these tools by listing these surveys, tools, and resources. Use your own discretion before participating.

ABOUT THE AUTHORS

SHAWN DOYLE, CSP

Shawn Doyle is a learning and development professional who has a passion for human potential. He is an avid believer in the concept of lifelong learning. For the last 23 years, Shawn has spent his time developing and implementing training programs on team building, communication, creativity, motivation, and leadership. He is the author of 14 books, and a Certified Speaking Professional. (Only 8 percent of speakers in the world are CSPs.) Shawn's company helps people become more effective in the workplace and in their lives. His clients include Pfizer, Comcast, Charter Media, IBM, Kraft, Microsoft, the US Marines, the Ladders, and Los Alamos National Defense Laboratory.

STEVEN ROWELL

Steven Rowell, former Disney leader/trainer, international speaker, author of four books, and business growth strategist, is known for his extraordinary creativity. Steven was former vice president, process excellence for Compass Group, and owner of Reconnect Consulting. Steven, with an M.A. in Organizational Effectiveness, is a proud father, husband, and raving fan of improv comedy, Goldendoodles, and Texas barbecue.